AF223838

The Astonishing Light of Your Own Being:

Powerful Practices to Shape Your Future and Showcase Your Brilliance

Copyright 2020, Starlene Justice. All rights reserved

Printed in the United States of America. No part of this publication may be reproduced, stored in a retrieval system, or transmitted by an means--electronic, mechanical, photographic (photocopying), recording, or otherwise--without prior permission in writing from the author.

Cover design by Robin Vuchnich

Interior design by Dino Marino

ISBN paperback: 978-1-7332104-2-3

ISBN eBook: 978-1-7332104-3-0

"One day the sun admitted

I am just a shadow.

I wish I could show you

The infinite incandescence

That has cast my brilliant image!

I wish I could show you,

When you are lonely or in darkness,

The Astonishing Light

Of your own Being!"

-Hafiz of Shiraz

This book is dedicated to my mother, Rev. Marynell Marsh.

She taught me that my thoughts matter, and that the world

holds beauty and wonder for those who will see.

TABLE OF CONTENTS

PART ONE:

POSSIBILITY

CHAPTER ONE

THE MEANING OF YOUR LIFE

*"Beauty is eternity gazing at itself in a mirror.
But you are eternity and you are the mirror."*

~Kahlil Gibran

It calls to you sometimes, doesn't it?

From the other side of the cliff where the waves rush upon the rocks. From the vaulted ceilings of ancient cathedrals, and the fragile spaces that exist between dreams and waking.

That feeling.

That feeling that tugs at you like a memory, but which can't be because you know you have never lived it. It's a feeling sometimes evoked by the strains of a certain melody; a feeling that lifts your heart out of your chest and expands your consciousness and occasionally blossoms into a visceral ache.

It's a feeling you can't name with certainty.

Sometimes you want to call it love.

Love of life, of the Universe, of *yourself* in a strange, uncertain way.

Sometimes you would call it gratitude. Reverence, perhaps.

It can even wear the cloak of loneliness and longing, mixed up with the desire to ease these things; and the suspicion that they *can* be eased, but you can't guess how.

It's a feeling of wondrous magic, of waiting, of something bubbling up inside you that clamors for attention. It's something you can't quite put your finger on, but something you want to try to hold onto.

It's a feeling that I will call "*possibility.*"

Does that seem right?

The *possibility* of being all that you *are.* The *possibility* of making good on your creative impulses, your most daring hopes, and the desires that spark and flame even without your conscious attention. The *possibility* of an extraordinary life; the life of your dreams.

We all have that feeling at some point. We all believe—usually when we are quite young—that everything we want will someday come to us, and we will be happy, contented, and fulfilled. It is as if we automatically and innately believe that it is our birthright; our destiny.

We know we are special; we know we are meant to shine. That is why we relinquish this dream with sadness. That is why we feel some measure of discomfort and distress when we *don't* shine. Because we were supposed to. We were born to do something; to *be* something.

We have always known it.

Isn't it so? Think about it. Think about your child-self. The dreams you had; the certainty that you only needed a little growing-up and all those things would be within your reach. As if your dreams were just apples hanging on a tree, and all you needed to reach them was a little more height.

So, you waited. And while you waited, you encountered disappointment, and struggle, and pain, and grief. You encountered your own perceived shortcomings and limitations. Worse, you encountered people who told you that your dreams were a function of your immaturity and that it was time to "grow up" and get "realistic." With sadness, you decided that dreams really were "dreams"; those shifting, misty specters which fade into falsehood in the cold light of morning.

What was it about life, or about living, that caused you to come to believe that the feeling that told you of your greatest potential was a feeling you had to keep under wraps, tucked into the deepest recesses of your heart?

It is something different for everyone: parents that were too harsh; a disability brought to light; the loss of love or respect from someone we felt we depended on utterly.

Perhaps, for many, it was just a fading away. The passing of years that brought new responsibilities and just as many reasons why it all might not turn out so wonderfully. Our dreams of the future—once supported by our assumptions surrounding adulthood and independence—were overtaken by the immediacy and challenge of simply surviving. Getting a job, buying food, paying the rent, figuring out transportation; these could all be wearyingly difficult.

And then, too, we started telling ourselves that our maturity gave us new insight; the ability to know that the dreams of our childhood were foolish, and that the role of the adult is to be responsible and practical. No need to feel guilty over dreams we bury and forget; we have *obligations* now.

And yet, there is still a world you are left wondering about, isn't there?

You can think of it as the hidden glade in a thick forest, where the grass is bright and lush—like looking out through freshly-washed windows—and where streams gurgle into crystal ponds teeming with shimmering trout. It's a view of the life you wish for, the life that flashes in front of your eyes from time to time, welling up from your depths like a submerged being and shedding pain off itself like water.

The only thing you can think to do is push it down. Again, and again.

You tell yourself that the pain you feel is hopelessness. The pain of losing that which your adult-self realizes you never had a chance of gaining in the first place. You believe that the only thing you are capable of figuring out now is a way to avoid that pain; a way to make your life *good enough*, even if it's never going to be great.

But I'm going to tell you something different.

I'm going to tell you that the pain you feel is not hopelessness but, rather, *hope*. This is what you can't tolerate. The worry niggling at the back of your mind that the life you've ended up with is an exact return on your investment, and that if you invested differently, you'd get different returns. The thought that maybe you *can* do the things you dream of, but you're not.

Why? Why have you silenced the calling of your highest self? Why have you relinquished the potential *you know you still have?*

For many people, it's a sense of duty, love for family (and believing our highest good is to put them first); responsibility; the desire to not appear selfish; illnesses or ailments outside our control; a physical appearance that doesn't lend itself to attracting affection. Insecurity, introversion, impoverishment, inability.

Maybe you believe that your job is not to *change* your circumstances, but just to make the best of them. You have the cards you were dealt, so carry on the best you can; keep a stiff upper lip. Don't complain. Even having hope is a bit like setting yourself up for disappointment; so long as you accept your fate, you avoid the pain of resistance, or effort, or failure.

These are all just a story. But because you are focused on what you see, you believe that story.

Sometimes they are an excuse; the thing you can point to for why your life doesn't look the way you wish it did. Who is to blame? How did you get to this spot?

It doesn't matter.

At some point you must face the fact that whatever or whomever brought you to the place you are at currently has no bearing on where you can, or will, or should go from here. Whatever ghetto, or prison, or hellhole you have been in, you can change your future. You are what you have occasionally believed yourself to be: a treasure, a miracle, an antidote to someone's poison, a light on the path, a gargantuan consciousness that holds within it the power to change lives, change worlds, change destiny.

Don't you know that? I think you do. I think we all have at least a tiny inkling of it, in our most honest moments.

Oh, but the burden it carries! To deliver on the promise of *who you are* takes courage, commitment, and a deep desire to come face-to-face with that person you've buried deep inside you.

What could that person do? *Who* could they be? What events could they put into motion, and how many lives could they impact? How would they feel? What would their life look like? What values, and characteristics, and emotions would they choose? Where would their path take them if they could genuinely listen to their heart's desires, own their authenticity and uniqueness, and pursue their highest calling?

There comes a moment when you *must* acknowledge that your future is up to you. That you are responsible for who and what you become from this point forward. That the past is just the past and the future is neither dependent on nor beholden to what came before. What is true, and what matters, is that the person you started out believing you could be is *still* the person you could be. It is your highest self.

What does that mean, though, to become one's highest self?

It would mean being the person that you would most like to be.

The person who knows what they love, what they're good at, and what they could create if they had no more excuses not to.

The person who brings value to self and others, and who acts boldly, courageously, kindly, and tenaciously.

The person who strives day to day, year to year, to improve their interactions, their relationships, their thoughts, and their deeds.

The person you catch a glimpse of from time to time who is funny, and talented, and confident, and who will joyfully and purposefully make their way in this seemingly crazy, drama-loving world.

That person who would hear and honor their inner voice and be willing to perform the excavations needed to unearth their authentic dreams and polish their finest traits.

That person you would choose to be if you could choose anyone at all, because you know it's who you really *are*.

How long has it been since you looked in the mirror and saw *that* person? Maybe never. But you know they exist. And when you have finally brought yourself—with care and consideration—into the fulfillment of that person who once seemed only to exist as a *possibility*, and when you have cultivated those characteristics that you now know to value, you will feel the sort of joy akin to unexpectedly encountering a long-lost friend in a strange land. "Is it really you?" you will say, as you grasp the beloved in a hug. "How *wonderful* to see you!"

But no one gets to their highest self by taking the escalator. There's a climb involved.

There's struggle, and pain, and risk, and insecurity, and fear.

This should not be viewed as some insurmountable obstacle, though. The battle, struggle, challenge—whatever you want to call it—to learn who we are and to honor who we are is no more difficult than living day to day as a false, downplayed version of ourselves. *Not* being authentic is hard. Going along to get along might seem like a good idea in the short term; avoid making waves; don't rock the boat. Over a lifetime, though, the losses mount. They come in the form of bitterness. Of depression. Of self-doubt and self-loathing. Or sometimes just complacency, and apathy, and resignation. Better to commit to the high, hard road that leads to an honest, fully engaged existence than to skate down Easy Street and find yourself in a purposeless, passionless hell. If you are going to feel insecurity, and pain, and fear (and no life is without these), then you might as well use them as currency toward your best life.

And this should not be understood as a means by which you gain worth as a human being. Whether a person fulfills their entire potential or not, aims higher or not, "succeeds" or not, they are a worthy human being. Worthy of their existence, worthy of a place in the world, worthy of love, and worthy of the freedom to determine their own destiny.

Worth is not earned; it is inherent.

But if you wish to achieve your greatest potential, and get in touch with your highest self, perhaps you just need to know how better to direct your actions. How to make manifest higher thoughts. And these things can be learned. This book you are holding in your hands is meant to be a guide along your path; to give you direction, and goals, and signposts.

You are bigger, and brighter, and bolder, and full of more power and possibility than you have ever imagined. You are a brilliant light and a special, sacred soul. Do you not know it?

The meaning of your life is to come to know it.

With this knowledge, you can embrace your unique attributes, and hone your finest talents. You can experience a life in tune to your deepest desires while increasing your capacity to share your greatest gifts with the world. And in so doing you can know the true joy of living the life you were meant to live.

CHAPTER TWO

THE ROLE OF BELIEF

"Don't you know it yet? It is your light that lights the worlds."

~Rumi

You are brilliant, you are genius; you are gods. You are powerful beyond measure. You can shape your own life; choose your own destiny; have whatever it is that you desire. Poets, sages, religious leaders, shamans, wisemen, and philosophers have tried to tell us this throughout all recorded history.

And year after year, decade after decade, age after age, we forget.

It is as if every new generation—no, every single, individual human being—must learn these things for themselves, as if they were the first in history. And without those to guide us, we would likely *never* learn it. It might seem improbable that such would be the case; that we would, somehow, be set up biologically to *forget* the very things that evolve and advance us.

And yet, consider the fact that without other humans to guide us, we would be utterly incapable of even basic survival.

Everything we know, we must learn from others.

We are not innately set up with the ability to survive and thrive. We are not physically strong, nor endowed with primal instincts or large fangs, nor are we especially fast or even able to walk for nearly the first full year of our lives. Without an immense amount of support for many years, we would all be doomed.

Without the help of other humans, survival *could* be possible under the most unusual and extraordinary circumstances (and a few such instances have been documented), but we could not, exactly, be human. So, it isn't, in fact, anomalous, that there is wisdom, knowledge, entire *ways of being* that would not be known unless they are deliberately taught by other humans.

The things you are going to learn—about bringing your finest being to light; about fulfilling your greatest promise; about sculpting your highest self—really do have to be *learned*.

You may want to believe that if such important knowledge were really true, and really necessary, we would already know how to access it, and how to perform the tasks associated with it. But I want to be clear that this is simply not the case.

Consider the following example:

If everyone who knew how to read and write and speak—in any language, it doesn't matter which—disappeared from the face of the earth in a cataclysmic event, and something akin to humanity somehow arose again from the ashes, how long would it take to relearn literacy, without anyone there to lead the way?

How long did it take the first time? Hundreds of years? Thousands? Hundreds of thousands? It is one of those anthropological questions without a definitive answer. And, yet, a human child who is *taught* these skills learns them readily and easily within their first ten (or so) years of life.

But it is easy to learn to read and write, isn't it? All around us, we see evidence that *it can be done*, and so even if, as little children, we find parts of it daunting, we never think to stop trying. We keep at it until we succeed. Because, after all, everyone around us seems perfectly capable of doing it.

So, there is a mental component at work here—a belief system, if you will—even if it is one of which we are not actively conscious.

We will readily achieve skillsets that are societally expected of us because, in part, we never consider *not* achieving them. Like walking. And talking. And reading and writing. We believe we will, and so we do. Even if, when we are learning to walk, we must fall down hundreds of times. And even if, when we are learning to write, we must be taught countless lessons about the language we have inherited, and we must practice, literally, for *years*. And yet, the vast majority of us succeed in this endeavor.

Now, this is not instinctual for us. There are instinctual *tendencies* around these things, and yet they must, without question, still be taught. We are highly social creatures and, as such, we rely on *society* (made up of other human beings) rather than *instinct* to teach us how to be human.

We are not born knowing; we must *learn*.

All of this is important to establish because, in essence, it sets up the following axioms:

First: that humans learn from other humans, and the things we are not taught may not come automatically to us. *Indeed, we may not even think of them at all.*

Second: that humans will achieve what they believe it is possible to achieve—usually based on the example set by others. Consider this:

What we see everyone doing, we all do.

What we see some people doing, we may consider doing, but we will have doubts.

What we see very few doing, we may view as impossible for ourselves.

And what we see no one doing, we proclaim to be impossible for humanity, at large.

But is it so? How many humans, in a vacuum of literacy, would dream up written language? How many would standardize and codify it? How many would even believe it was possible? Who would even *conceptualize* it? It *isn't* all that easy. And yet, because we, as a species, accept it as real and possible, it *is* real and possible for us all.

The other important thing to realize from this example is that even the things we all expect to be able to do as humans—walk, talk, write—take a great deal of practice. Think how easily we are prone to giving up when someone suggests we need to practice having better thoughts, visualizing different outcomes, creating a brilliant life. As if the difficulty in achieving these things makes them not even worthy of our basic consideration.

Are there other things out there—creative processes, ways of being, cognitive pursuits, intellectual and physical capacities—that if we were taught how to access them, and if we believed they were possible, would become as easy and as important to humanity as written language?

I believe so, but not everyone does. And therein lies part of the problem. In the opening paragraph of this chapter, I invoked all the brilliant minds of the past who have asserted that humanity has within its grasp an astonishingly creative genius: *the ability to shape reality to suit its desires.* I suggested that we have repeatedly forgotten this. I think, however, that it is even more strange and more insidious than a simple forgetting; I think we don't *believe.* And as I attempted to establish with the example of basic human skillsets, believing that we can do something is critical to being able to do it.

Consider the following words from wise people across the ages:

"If thou canst believe, all things are possible to him that believeth."
Jesus. Mark 9:23.

"Man often becomes what he believes himself to be."
Mahatma Gandhi

"Man is made by his beliefs. As he believes, so he is."
Johann Wolfgang von Goethe

*"The thing always appears that you really believe in;
and the belief in a thing makes it happen."*

Frank Lloyd Wright

*"The outer conditions of a person's life will always be found
to reflect their inner beliefs."*

James Allen

I could go on for many lines; many pages, even. But what is the reader's experience of these passages as he or she scans through them? Do they sink in deeply? Or do you skim past them, their meaning already diffused by the sheer repetition? These things *sound* good, but they can't be *true*, can they?

But what if they *were* true? *And true at face value.*

Go back and read them. Think about it.

Have we really forgotten our own power in our ability to shape our destiny? Or is it a failure of *belief?* At a fundamental level, we don't believe we have the capacity to create the lives of our dreams, and to wield the inherent power of consciousness and thought to produce whatever results we desire.

Whether it's a failure of memory or a failure of mindset, there are, thankfully, those who would remind us. And exhibit in their own lives the truth of this reality. And until we take for granted our abilities of thought and creation in the same way we take for granted our ability to learn language and write, these reminders will be necessary.

I titled this section "Possibility" because this is the first thing I want you to consider. I want you to wipe the slate of your mind clean and consider how you could change your life if you focused on possibility rather than impossibility. If you did it literally, deliberately, and daily.

We are surrounded by evidence that things that once seemed impossible are, in fact, wholly possible: airplanes, cell phones, televisions, artificial intelligence, self-driving cars, manned space flight, buildings that create their own energy, artificial leaves (a potential bounty of renewable energy), satellites that use invisible light to gather data and render images on computer screens, and so on.

How did these things come to be? Did they happen by accident? Were they a mere "discovery" that someone chanced upon? Of course not. Someone thought them up—some person. Someone created an image in their mind, and a vision of a future that did not, at the time, exist, and they moved forward with that image and that vision as a guiding light. And they did it because they *believed* that the fulfillment of that vision was possible. Not simple. Not easy. Just possible.

And let me mention that not everything deemed impossible by any given person is as far-out and innovative as the examples I have just offered.

You may believe it is impossible to become a millionaire—even though millionaires are made every day—or even secure a job that pays a living wage. You may believe it's impossible for someone amazing to fall madly in love with you and want to marry you. Or that it's not possible—indeed, perfectly acceptable—to make a really good living doing something you love and are passionate about. There are many of us who secretly, subconsciously believe that the things we are inherently good at and like to do are meant to be our *hobbies* only, and the thing we make a living at has been based on a whole different set of imperatives; duty, responsibility, security. Because *that's just the way it is.*

It is not because these things themselves seem so impossible; they simply seem impossible to *some people.* Henry Ford once said, "Whether you think you can, or think you can't, you're right." It's not the *thing* (or the accomplishment, or the state-of-being), it's *what you think about it.*

What are the beliefs you hold about your own life?

Think about this for a moment. It really *does* take conscious thought because we often don't see these things as beliefs; we see them as our circumstances or our reality.

Do you believe that because you grew up poor, and didn't go to college, and had children at a young age that your potential is capped at a low level beyond which you will not be able to rise?

The *not being able to rise part* is not a result of those circumstances; it's a result of what you believe those circumstances mean for you. Even if you have not consciously articulated those beliefs.

What I want to teach you is that most of us have got that continuum backwards: we think that our beliefs are created by our reality; in fact, we can change our reality by changing our beliefs.

Do you believe you are unattractive? Do you believe you are not very smart? Do you believe that getting a good job that pays the bills and puts food on the table is the best you can expect from your life? Do you believe you are too old to start school, too young to start a business, too insecure to stretch your limits, too impatient to become a teacher, too selfish to become a parent, too sick to ever get well, too obligated to ever be free?

What you *believe*, is what *is*.

The "realistic" person may be railing that this is fundamentally impossible, that we no more control what happens to us through our thoughts and beliefs than we control whether the skies rain upon us or the sun shines.

And what I'm saying is: *yes, we do.*

And this is what Jesus said, and Buddha, and Gandhi, and good ol' Henry Ford.

You have not thought of all the things you can do; all the ways you can be. You look out through your eyes and see a world that you think is unchangeable, forgetting that it's your mind that translates what your eyes see, and that the change you want is only a "vision" away. You let disadvantages form permanent barriers that stop your forward momentum, as if you are not perfectly capable of miracles.

That box you live in; you built it. And you continuously construct the same box around yourself while seeming to move along.

"I tried this," you might say.

"I can't do that."

"I'm not like you."

"I have obstacles to overcome that you can't even imagine."

What you *believe*, is what *is*.

If you believe the circumstances of your life are what determine the possibility of your life, then that will be your reality. If you believe that the circumstances of your life are only the setting, the stage, the background scenery for whatever you *choose* to do, then *that* will be your reality.

What is your vision of your life and the world at large? (Believe me, you have one. And you should take a good, hard look at it).

As you go through each day, what is your dominant state of being? Stressed? Anxious? Angry? Excited and engaged? Blessed and grateful?

Are you even aware?

What are the thoughts that flit through your subconscious, like wild birds scrabbling around a feeder, vying for your attention?

Or maybe these thoughts are skulking, like a predator, looking for an unlocked window. An accidental invitation.

Are you a person who sees others' lives as brilliant and your own life as a faded, trampled-on banner? Maybe you hung it high once and flew it proudly, but failures came along. And rejection. And pain. And crises of health, and belief, and ability, and achievement.

Somewhere along the way, all the heroes' tales you wanted to be a part of got replaced with feelings of failure and hopelessness—or just plain humdrum mediocrity. Now the stories are all about what's *not* possible, and what you know you *can't* do, and how the world we live in has nothing pure, or beautiful, or hopeful, or inspirational, or encouraging, or bright to offer anymore.

There are wars, political infighting, rampant societal violence, motivations of greed, and status-quo, and privilege. There is disease, and toxins in the environment, and depletion of natural resources, and destruction of habitat. Hell, no one even writes good books or makes good movies anymore. (Admit it; you've probably said those last things yourself!).

The economy is broken, the poor have no chance, education is too expensive, our food is poisoned, and your parents taught you nothing except how to be afraid.

Why bother trying?

We have been brainwashed into believing that it's a sick and twisted world, and that humanity is barely keeping its head above water, let alone thriving.

As perhaps the only creature who is self-determining, this belief has got to be taking a toll on us.

What if *the truth* is that our capacity for goodness, for creativity, for productivity is far greater than we have ever imagined and that, because we are blind to this truth, we lower our expectations and sell ourselves short? And what if the limitations we choose to put on ourselves are nothing more than that: *choices?* And what if we could choose differently?

What if, by changing your perspective, you could see a world that is radically different; full of choices that can be customized perfectly by you, to serve you? Would you do it? And if you could see it, and believe that it's real and focus on the good, how would that change what you think of *yourself?* Would you have hope? Would you do things differently?

What if you believed you were a crucial component of the building of a brilliant world? What if the "darkness" you perceive is actually riddled with cracks ready to burst apart and release the light of all the ages? What if the Universe was just waiting for those who would believe that there is a different future and a different human potential than the one we have been coerced into taking for granted? What if our perspectives are really like a transmitter, and what we perceive is cause and consequence of the type of energy we transmit?

If all these things were so, *what would you do differently?*

This is going to be hard for some readers to accept, and there may be those among you who will toss the book aside after reading it, but I will say it anyway. It is this: if you don't believe you can ever be in different circumstances than the ones you are in, *then you cannot be.*

By the same token, if our reality is shaped primarily by our beliefs, then the obstacles to changing our circumstances are mainly in our minds. How astonishing that mankind has been taught this truth for, literally, thousands of years and yet we act as if we are still looking for the key to become exactly who we want to be.

The key is this: what you think, you become. What you focus on expands to fill a greater part of your awareness. What you believe, you see (and not the other way around). And there is only one way to prove all of this: you have to try it on. You have to commit to doing it.

CHAPTER THREE

YOU CAN DO IT WHEN YOU THINK YOU CAN

"Man often becomes what he believes himself to be. If I keep on saying to myself that I cannot do a certain thing, it is possible that I may end by really becoming incapable of doing it. On the contrary, if I shall have the belief that I can do it, I shall surely acquire the capacity to do it, even if I may not have it at the beginning."

~ Mahatma Gandhi

It is not farfetched, really; this idea that the belief comes before the reality, and not the reverse. If our beliefs inform our actions, then by changing our beliefs, we may take different actions, which will lead to different results, which will then lead to a different reality.

Or even if the belief simply informs our subconscious, and our subconscious acts on our internal world in terms of expectations, we can have different outcomes because of the interconnectivity of thought, feeling, perception, and behavior.

You've heard of a self-fulfilling prophecy, right? This notion that when we make a claim about ourselves, the simple fact of us having planted that seed and watered it frequently with our thoughts, will make the thing more likely to happen.

The problem here—and the way we normally think of a "self-fulfilling prophecy"—is that these are not usually positive things. They are almost always negative.

For example, before a big test, we might say (to ourselves or even out loud to someone else), "I'm way too nervous for this; I'm totally going to choke. There's no way I can pass this thing." And what happens? We get nervous, the nervousness shuts down our brain, we panic, we forget everything, we flunk.

"I knew it," we say, with resignation. "I told you so."

Self-fulfilling prophecy.

But does it work in the reverse, too? Can you say, or think, or believe something positive and have *that* become your reality?

Well, of course.

Do you believe intelligence is fixed or malleable?

Do you believe personality traits are fixed or malleable?

Do you believe skillsets and aptitudes are fixed or malleable?

Here is the astonishing thing that research has shown: if you believe certain things are fixed, you are more likely to prove this "truth" in your own life; if you believe they are malleable (what Carol Dweck calls a "growth mindset" in her fantastic book, *Mindset*), then you are more likely to prove *that* "truth." A person who is not good at math, but who believes that they can get *better*, will, in fact, get better. A person who believes that their inaptitude for math is set in stone will *not* tend to get better. (Often because they won't try to get better; they simply don't believe it's possible).

I'm a geography teacher, so in my world, rather than hearing the old mantra, "I'm not good at math," what I hear is, "I'm not good at *maps*."

I have heard this said countless times, and I still find it amusing that anyone would think that there's a specific aptitude for it; that one is either good or not good at *maps*. It may be true that some students have a harder time with the spatial aspect of maps, which does require a different way of thinking than most of them are probably accustomed to, or maybe have even been exposed to. But in most cases, it's not that they're not good at maps; it's that they are simply not experienced in using them. Since they have written off their potential in this area, however, because of a prior belief, they don't even try to get better. They don't attempt different strategies; they don't ask for help; they don't spend more time on the subject—which is exactly what they *should* do if it is not one of their professed strengths. They simply throw up their hands. As if they are helpless. As if the statement, "I'm not good at maps" was a pronouncement sent down from God-Almighty and is not to be questioned or challenged.

We do this all the time in multiple areas of our lives across the decades.

We may even bypass opportunities, or settle for lower levels of education, or sacrifice our hopes and dreams in their entirety because we are absolutely certain there is this one, little obstacle we can't overcome.

There may even be some part of our subconscious minds that holds onto these obstacles like a lifeboat. They keep us safe. They let us off the hook. They give us a reasonable pretext for why we didn't do the things we wanted to do.

Does this happen to you?

Without really thinking about it, you may offer up seemingly valid reasons to yourself and others for why you didn't challenge yourself, or why you stayed stuck in a dead-end job, or why the place you've ended up is *just as well, anyway.* Your anxiety. Your addictions. Your financial fears. Your awkwardness around people. Your struggles with technology. Your difficulty with math. Your special-needs child you have to care for. Your domineering spouse who won't "let" you.

Are these some of the things you've been telling yourself? Take some time over the next few weeks to observe it. Listen closely and carefully to the stories you tell. To other people and to yourself. Are they really true; these limiting beliefs that you have let shape your choices? Are you using them to avoid taking the hard path that will lead you to your better life?

While it is comfortable and safe to stay where you are, it is only in making changes, taking action, and moving forward that we get to the life we long for; the life we believe is possible in moments of honest reckoning.

The truth is, a person who is determined, motivated, and confident will have come to see obstacles differently. Even if these things really are weak points. And I'm not saying that people don't have such weak points—they do. We all do. We all are blessed with things we do better than other things. But that doesn't make the other things *impossible*; it just makes them harder.

To be sure, I am of the belief that the things we are drawn to, and have a natural propensity for, are our greatest gifts, and that if we focus on these *strengths*—giving them priority over the things we struggle more with—we will go farther, faster. But sometimes we *must* develop skill sets in things we consider weaknesses in order to maximize the value of our strengths.

For example, any student needing to conquer the stuff they struggle with in order to get a degree in the subject in which they shine. This is the case in many fields of study: nursing, psychology, architecture, engineering, accounting, and on and on.

When you come to a place where you're called on to do these things that are *hard*, that's when you have to pull out all the stops, dig deep, and come up with some grit. Practicing this is also what will put you on the path to becoming those three descriptors I mentioned above: determined, motivated, and confident—if you do not think of yourself in these terms already. Have compassion for yourself in this process. It can take time. It requires learning and practice.

Humans are tremendously resilient, and we should give ourselves credit for this. Most of the time, people give up on things way too quickly and way too easily. Don't shame yourself for your failures when they happen; learn and move forward.

Why does a baby continue trying to walk even when it falls constantly and is thwarted repeatedly? Because that baby is *motivated*. And it sees everyone around it get what they want by standing up and walking.

Obviously, this is how reality works. At some point the baby feels trapped in its lowly, slow world while every day, all around it, magic is happening. So many things to see and do and taste and try. So many *possibilities*. It is not fenced-in by the limitations of its own mind yet. It knows only that there is something it desires, there is clearly a way to get it, and it will do whatever it takes to fulfill that desire. It just has to keep trying over and over. What's the big deal?

What caused us to stop being the way we were when we were babies?

I think that at some point we started to *internalize* our failures; we started thinking they meant something was wrong with us; that we were not all that we could be or should be. Rather than taking our falls in stride—as just part of the learning process—we started to believe that they meant something about us, about who we are, and what we're capable of.

No longer did we feel comfortable trying and trying until we figured something out. Somehow, we learned that the very act of *trying* meant that we weren't very good, and that made us feel vulnerable or less-than.

What if we could all happily fail as we went about the beautiful business of learning something new, or figuring out something that is hard for us? Or what if we simply believed that, overall, we are capable of most things we might want to take on? We wouldn't let ourselves be stopped by limiting beliefs.

The whole world would open up.

Many of us have heard of the study done where a teacher was told that her class was full of brilliant students, and so she taught them as if they were brilliant, and they performed magnificently. Turned out, they were students who had only tested as average, initially. Her expectations (which were seemingly intangible) had a profound influence on the outcomes that those students achieved. Her elevated expectations had a profound influence on the outcomes those students achieved. They noticed that she set the bar high, and they believed that she would not do that if it were not possible for them to reach it. So, dutifully, they reached it.

For the unfamiliar, I would like to point out that there are numerous studies linking thought/expectation/belief and measurable outcomes in various fields or categories (the most famous probably being the placebo effect, where the mere *belief* that a drug would improve a condition was as powerful as the drug itself). Since there are plenty of books that detail this information (the aforementioned one by Carol Dweck is a great one), I don't need to belabor the point here. What I would prefer to do is to suggest how best you might use it.

Because the trick, you see, is in taking action that reflects a particular belief *even if that belief is not even formed yet.*

I don't mean that the *thought* isn't formed yet—obviously, you have to think it before you can believe it—just that we often have thoughts, or we are told to encourage thoughts, that we don't actually believe. But it's important to have those thoughts in order to eventually get to the belief. In a very simplistic sense—and something I did early on in what I will describe as my "evolution"—we develop our ability to make choices in alignment with what we *wish* to believe, rather than with what we *do* believe.

For example: suppose you are a student. Suppose you are a student at the beginning of your higher educational experience; perhaps taking some classes at a community college. Suppose your belief about yourself is that you are a mediocre student with limited talents and abilities, but you think that getting a degree will at least move the dial a little with regard to the potential your life represents.

Typically, a student like this will hedge their bets. They will choose a path of study that represents what they think they can accomplish, and a transfer university that they believe they can easily get into.

They will not take a moment to envision their *ideal* scenario.

They will not peruse the websites of high-end universities.

They will not ask themselves what they would like to be, *if they could be anything at all.*

In other words, they will choose their future based on their past, and based on the beliefs they currently hold about themselves.

But what if they shook up this model?

I will let you consider this for yourself.

What do you suppose would happen if just such a student decided to go off the rails a bit? Let's say they have an interest in astronomy, but they have always told themselves that there are no jobs in astronomy and, anyway, they're not good at math. They wouldn't even consider choosing this field as their major. Better to go with what they view as an "easier" science like psychology, and just take a few astronomy classes on the side— to assuage their curiosity and allow them to indulge in a guilty pleasure.

But after their first class in astronomy, they feel enlivened, awakened, eager, and they take a curiously radical step: they decide to major in astronomy.

They feel a rightness in this decision, and the new desire like a rush of adrenaline. They feel challenged, stoked, lit-up. Their beliefs about themselves are exactly the same at this point—but they have allowed a new thought to enter.

Keep in mind, they are not going through this process deliberately or consciously. The student has been inspired by something (their first astronomy class, in this case) and feels motivated and excited. The fact that they have been trapped by old thought patterns and want to be trapped no longer may not occur to them at all. Regardless, those patterns have probably been there, and are now going to get challenged.

So, the next thing that happens is that they start looking at universities that offer degrees in this "crazy" field, and as they read through all the requirements, their chest tightens, and a knot forms in the pit of their stomach, and they shut down the computer and say, "Never mind; it's too hard."

Those old, engrained beliefs don't just go away.

What you can see here, though, is that something has been set into motion, so even though the old beliefs want to nudge their way back in, something has shifted. The seed has been sown. Somewhere deep in their subconscious a new belief about themselves is taking shape. The belief that they *could* do this. Now, the idea of *not* doing it is so disappointing that they feel themselves to be at a crossroads: go back to their original plan and desperately subdue and erase that subversive passion that had arisen so abruptly and unexpectedly or decide that—come hell or high water—they are going to pursue the thing that really matters to them.

I am going to predict that some of my readers are thinking, "That's a no-brainer! They should pursue the thing that really matters to them." And other readers are thinking, "That would be the dumbest thing they ever did. Talk about hanging yourself out over an abyss." There's a bit of both of those readers in all of us, I would wager.

You can begin to see, though, how the things that could be opportunities, or pathways for growth can turn into points of pain when they get downplayed and shut out.

How many times, and in how many scenarios, have you played it safe? Believe it or not, most of the time people *won't* pursue something like what I have illustrated in the above scenario.

In fact, again and again, in multiple situations throughout our lives, we shut down those interests that rise up within us and then justify this choice with a list of reasons we consider foolish to ignore.

In a way, this is not an unreasonable response. Our "outlandish" ideas, while attractive in some respects—especially in the way they excite our interest—also lead to deep discomfort when we begin to analyze exactly what would be needed to follow such a path. We feel *compelled*, almost, to shut them down in order to save ourselves from stepping out on a path that fills us with wobbly-legged fear and infringes on all our comfort zones.

We listen to the voice in our head (and sometimes to the voices of well-meaning friends and family) that our chosen field of study is not going to yield any jobs, or that it will cost too much, or that we'll get burnt out before we can even make a dent in all the hard science and math, or that the thing that has excited us is just a phase, just a distraction, or meant to be just a hobby.

Indeed, it's quite possible that you are—right now—running through all the reasons in your head why there is absolutely nothing wrong with these justifications. In a sensible world, and from a sensible standpoint, they would be meaningful. But if it's *the thing that really matters*, sense has got nothing to do with it. Will that reason be meaningful on your death bed? That you made the "sensible" choice?

It is startling how willing we are to relinquish the deepest desires of our hearts, and the most innate cravings of our consciousness for reasons that we don't even question all that deeply.

But let's get back to our student. What if *this* particular student decides to go through with it? What do you think the outcome will be once they have mapped out an educational plan that includes their number one choice of career (if they are willing to entertain that "in a perfect world" scenario), and their number one choice of university, if they can convince themselves that this is even remotely within the realm of possibility?

My friends, they will move heaven and earth. And you know it. Not all at once, of course. But bit by bit, step by step, challenge by challenge. Chipping away at one obstacle, and then the next, until the fulfillment of the dream becomes not merely a possibility, but an *inevitability*.

Isn't it amazing?

How we bring so many skills and talents to bear *when we have decided that something is possible*. How energized we feel when we go after something *we really want* rather than being "realistic," "sensible," or just taking the path of least resistance. (Those descriptors are in quotes because I believe that it is, ultimately, both realistic *and* sensible to follow our dreams).

And this is what I mean about acting as if you believed a certain way, *even before you really believe it*. In the case of the student, they did not believe they were cut out for a "hard" field of study, but they started researching it, and moving in that direction from pure curiosity, interest, and passion. It is likely that, eventually, they will completely change their belief about what is possible. Or, indeed, about what they might view as "realistic" and "sensible"!

In this theoretical case I am referencing here, the leap from "impossible" to "possible" happened as a result of the student methodically taking steps in the direction of a desired reality until those steps, slowly but surely, strengthened their nascent hopes and reinforced their choices. Eventually—almost as if by accident—they are in possession of a different set of beliefs about their life than they were ever in possession of before. And this sort of thing can happen even without deliberation or conscious choice in the matter.

But what I would like to make apparent, is that you can do this *consciously*. Once you know that changing your beliefs is simply a matter of engineering your circumstances to be supportive of your choices and your vision (one step at a time), you realize that it is possible to change your beliefs *before* you even take those steps. When you know how this works, you can change anything you want to in your life.

One of the ways I saw this play out in my own life was when I was working on a memoir-like story for a writing contest that had been brought to my attention. The entrance requirement was a novel-length manuscript by a certain deadline (which was only about 6 weeks away), and it just so happened that I needed to do this while I was teaching a summer class (which meant the class met every day for long hours because the semester was very short) on a topic *I had never taught before*. So, not only was I creating my lectures and assignments on a day-to-day basis, I was also trying to write a book.

When I first considered taking this on, I shook my head and told myself I was crazy. In fact, I told more than just myself. I told my mother, who was the one who pointed out this contest to me in the first place. And in addition to professing my lunacy to anyone who would listen, I began to create a mental checklist of everything I could use to support that verdict. Heaven forbid I am not utterly convinced of the idiocy of this idea that tugged at me.

But just like the student in the previous example, a fire had been lit in me—a deep desire to see if I *could* manage to get something ready for this contest. If I took a moment to think about it, I would say that it wasn't just that I was motivated by the challenge itself, but by the fact that it was such a *difficult* challenge. Maybe because I knew that if I took it on and failed, no one would judge me. (Except for being crazy enough to take it on in the first place—but I had already told myself that line).

More likely, though, it was the fact that for anyone to be motivated by something, they have to see the challenge as being worthy of their effort. This is why schoolchildren will often perform better with a more difficult curriculum. *The difficulty itself is a motivator.* I think we forget about this sometimes when we are setting up challenges for ourselves. Fearing to set the bar too high, we may inadvertently set it too low and miss out on one of the ways by which we could be inspired and motivated.

In addition to these factors, I could tell that this writing challenge was something important to me; important to *who I was*, at a very fundamental level. It was a challenge that resonated for me. Just like the student who took the astronomy class.

As predicted, the workload was incredibly heavy. There were many times when I wanted to give up; when I told myself that I couldn't handle it. But then I discovered a little trick; such a simple way of shifting my thoughts and my energy. When I got tired or frustrated, I would just say, out loud, "I can do this."

I said it over and over.

When getting up early to write was wearing thin, and all the grading and material prep I was doing kept me busy well into the night.

When the words in my story barely reached 100 on some days, and I needed to hit over 20,000 in total.

When I had no idea what to write but sat down anyway and hoped something would come.

When my mom apologized for ever mentioning the contest because she worried I was running myself into the ground trying to make the deadline.

"I can do this."

I said it not because I believed it, but because I wanted to *come to believe it*. Because if I could believe it, then I could make it happen. And, in the end, I did.

I even ended up being a finalist in that contest.

It also turned out to be the catalyst for getting me back into writing, which had been my dream since I was seven years old. I had let it fall by the wayside because I had told myself it was "too hard" with kids to raise and a teaching career to build.

By using the mantra, "I can do this," I was practicing what is classically called an "affirmation"—a statement that reinforces an idea we want to buy into.

For me, the power was in the fact that the thing I was trying to do was not some random challenge that didn't matter one way or another; it was something that excited me, and that felt meaningful. It was also something I really wasn't sure I could do. I literally felt like I needed to encourage myself with those words, even though I didn't exactly believe them at first. I needed to shut out the negative comments that ran through my head and direct my focus in a very singular fashion—much like a person meditating will focus on their breath, or a certain word.

The truth is, we can do more than we think we can. We can go farther; we can last longer; we can do things better; we can accomplish more. Henry Ford said, "There is no man living who isn't capable of doing more than he thinks he can do."

To be sure, affirmations do not create magic. Although it may feel that way, at times. I still wrote the book. I still taught my class. I didn't bring in a substitute to cover half the semester, and I didn't have little elves sneaking into my room and working on my manuscript in the middle of the night. But if I hadn't worked at changing my foundational beliefs about what I could or couldn't do with that little statement I kept telling myself, then I probably would not have accomplished that task. Those words, "I can do this," became a self-fulfilling prophecy; a positive one.

When you change the way you think in order to create a different belief, you will take additional action in congruence with that belief. As this happens, there is the possibility of progress or success which, in turn, reinforces your action taken, creates confidence, and builds momentum. In the end, you will see your reality change as you develop a more comprehensive system of beliefs about what is possible for you.

And you can do this again and again.

But, interestingly, it isn't just the *action* that changes the reality. The thoughts and beliefs, *themselves*, also have a hand in this. Let's explore this further.

CHAPTER FOUR

CREATING A VISION AND CHOOSING YOUR ENERGY CHANNEL

"Change your thoughts and you change your world."

~Norman Vincent Peale

In addition to the concept of "belief," there are two others that I want to throw into the mix: "faith," and "vision." You may be inclined to think of these as abstract ideas with no concrete reality, but I would argue that they are the very foundation and pathway for all meaningful achievement.

When I first started working on this book, I had the thought that I would separate out these concepts and give each of them their own, individual treatment. But then I realized that they are not exactly separate things; they are different parts of the *same* thing. They work together like interlocking gears. One does not stand alone or function without the others.

Consider faith, for example, which is complete trust or confidence in something. How does one arrive at such a place? It comes from a very deep belief—in one's ability or in what is possible. But where does the belief come from to begin with?

It is born from a recurring vision, and nurtured with consistent, deliberate choices and actions.

Having a vision of what you want can create a belief that your vision will come true. When you believe it strongly enough—while reinforcing it with consistent, directed action—you can then be said to have faith. And faith remains against all evidence of a contrary nature.

If I could name which of these is the most important, I would say it is faith. Because faith becomes the force that outlasts your weakening willpower or your disabled discipline. It allows you to persevere in the face of even the greatest obstacles. To rewrite, re-wire, re-invent, if you must. Or even to simply rest.

And without a clear vision, without belief, in what would we have faith? This is why it is necessary to address them together. If we take them apart, they lose their integrity. It would be like whisking the earth away from the sun and expecting natural processes to work the same way they always have. Without the sun heating the surface unevenly, the air at the surface wouldn't rise, and cool, and condense, and create clouds. There would be no warmth, no rain, no photosynthesis, no plants, no animals, no wind, no light, and so on. All these parts rely on each other—like interlocking gears—and the sun is the powerhouse that runs it all.

So, what is the powerhouse that runs the machinery that creates our thoughts, our dreams, our goals, our beliefs, and our ambitions?

I indicated that *faith* was the most important of the interlocking gears, but it's the intended outcome, not the starting point. The starting point is your vision. The vision you have of your own life.

If you haven't created a deliberate vision, then I can promise you that you have been running on a default one. There is no such thing as not having any vision at all. The real issue is: did you *choose* the vision you see of your life, or did you let circumstances (or society) choose it for you?

The events and experiences that put in place whatever vision guides your thoughts about your life up to this point may be fair game for scrutiny. It may even be useful to tease out precisely which circumstances created which part of the vision. But not right now. I don't want anything to distract you from the most important thing. Starting this very moment, you can (and *must*) begin to create a vision of the life *you want*. It is critically important that you *see* yourself inhabiting the life of your dreams.

No more default visions; you are going to choose every component of your life.

And why not?

What are your dominant beliefs, and how do they shape the vision you will allow for yourself? For example, you may have already started to think about what you want your life to look like. And you may have found that you run up against some blockades almost instantly. Maybe you started off thinking, "Oh, I want to be rich!" and then you quickly dialed it back down with the thought: "Well, I don't have to be *rich*, but I would like to not have to worry about money. If I could just pay off this house that I live in, that would be fine. Maybe a little extra money to travel once in a while."

What? Really?

You've just rubbed a magic lamp, the genie has appeared, and this is what you are going to ask of it?

Look, honey, you don't have to *believe* it. Not yet. But for crying out loud don't start limiting yourself at the imagination stage. I'm saying this because I know you probably will. Oh, not just you. Me, too. Everyone is in danger of self-limiting beliefs. Both in how we view what is possible for ourselves, and what is possible (or acceptable) out in the world.

Consider the great painter, Pablo Picasso. What if he told himself that the type of artwork he wanted to create was not something that would ever be accepted by the art world, or the art-loving public? What if he shut off his talent, certain that he was destined to fail? Or what if he believed that even *being an artist* was not a reasonable or appropriate choice? (He did *not* believe this at all, of course, and was absolutely comfortable and confident in his right and ability to live the exact life he chose).

Don't get discouraged, though, if you *do* have a tendency to limit yourself. I remember the first time I read Toni Morrison's novel, *Beloved*, and being shocked to my foundations that she actually wrote a novel of literary fiction in which the ghost of a baby inhabited a house and even caused the house to pitch and roll at times. I thought this sort of artistic license was against the rules—not allowed by the "powers that be" in literary fiction. Blew away all my preconceived notions about what is possible in writing, and the literal and figurative places you can go when you don't automatically censor your own vision. Thank goodness *she* didn't believe such a way of writing was impossible! So, as Toni Morrison did to such great effect, let your imagination run wild.

Because, you see, *you start to change your belief systems just by changing what you envision.* And when you start moving toward that vision, you create new belief systems. And once you change your beliefs, you are well on your way to creating a foundation of solid faith.

Before I understood how faith worked, I wanted to wrest it from my consciousness by force; strong-arm it out of the ether. I figured it was something I could conjure if I pretended hard enough. Like maybe I could fool the Universe. After all, it felt like faith was something I should have, and if I didn't, I suppose I felt that it hinted at something unformed, immature, certainly flawed or lacking.

What I came to realize later is that faith is part of a bigger process; *it's what you arrive at* when you walk through the other things; when you work on the other pieces. It is developed over time because of what you do, and how you think, and who you become as a result of all these processes. It grows organically out of your changing visions, actions, and beliefs.

I think this is wonderful. It lets us off the hook if we start off *without* enough faith; we know we can come around to that place, eventually, where we are genuinely experiencing it.

But belief comes before faith, and to get to belief when you don't have it requires nothing more than a set of strategies. At the heart of this strategizing is a curiously unique human property: the ability to imagine in our minds something that does not yet exist in front of us. In other words, the ability to *envision.*

Humans are naturally and inherently imaginative. It is a defining feature of childhood. We never lose our ability to imagine things, but we do change the ways in which we use that ability.

Children conjure things deliberately and for the sake of their own pleasure. Adults have a tendency to imagine drama (how you're going to tell off your boss if they chastise you again about that late project), things they are afraid of (which creates feelings of anxiety and worry), and mind-movies about the things they anticipate the day will hold (which is fine, except that these mind-movies are mostly based on past experiences, are not actively *creative,* and are very often negative).

Research has shown that people have the ability to influence the outcome of something by first imagining their *intended* outcome. This has been measured in athletes, perhaps most famously, who have pictured their event in their mind—going over how the race, or game, or competition will play out—and practicing the winning moves.

You may have done something similar yourself in the past—like, say, for a job interview or a date. Not surprisingly, picturing negative situations (questions you can't answer for the interview, or being overly worried if your date will like you and imagining what will happen if they don't) will create nervousness and anxiety that will undermine confidence. And undermining your confidence is *not* something you want to do in your quest for success.

This, however, is just a very shallow explanation of why good thoughts produce good outcomes, and bad thoughts produce bad outcomes. (Especially if these are part of a person's overall make-up and character over a long period of time). It goes much deeper than that.

Let's get back to the example of the sun that I used earlier.

All day and all night, day after day, year after year, millennium after millennium, the nuclear reactions of the sun are creating waves of energy that burst forth from that gaseous ball of fire, hurtle themselves through space, and eventually strike the earth. The earth, too, is emitting energy of its own. In fact, *all things* emit energy. We call this energy electromagnetic radiation. Everything emits it. If an object is very hot, some of that energy will appear as light (the sun, for example), and if the object is cooler, the energy will manifest differently. What distinguishes these different types of energy is their wavelength. The spectrum of electromagnetic radiation is, essentially, infinite, but we do have interactions with a small portion of it. The light we see, the light we don't see (infrared and ultraviolet, for example), x-rays, gamma rays, radio waves, microwaves, and so on.

Consider those last few for a moment. Think what we can do with these components of the electromagnetic spectrum. It's rather stunning, actually. Seeing inside a person without cutting them open; cooking food without fire; sending messages via signals that we cannot see or hear or feel, but which we can transmit and receive with the right equipment.

If we didn't know any better, we'd think it was pure magic.

How long have we been aware of these possibilities and used them? A hundred years, give or take?

What do you suppose we still *don't know*?

One of my favorite quotes from T.S. Eliot is: "All our knowledge brings us nearer to our ignorance." The more we know, the more we know we don't know. How wonderful! How exciting! How hopeful to realize that! It means that there is always something to learn and know, and that long-standing issues have potential solutions that haven't even been dreamed of yet.

So, guess what? *You* are emitting electromagnetic radiation, as well. You, and me, and your dogs, and your boss, and that person you really want to date.

Do you honestly think that all that information that is being sent out of our bodies at certain wavelengths is going undetected by anything else? Without a proper transmitter and receiver, no one could hear a radio or watch a television. But *with* that capability, the amount of information that can be transmitted and received is infinite.

What information are we sending out into the wild blue yonder? And who (or what) is receiving it?

No one?

Don't count on it.

I believe that *everyone* is receiving it. It might even be said that the Universe, at large, is receiving it. We are not always in tune to the energy out there. Certainly, we have all had the experience of being *more* in tune to some people or things than others. Like a radio, there are different wavelengths of available information. We can tune in, and we can tune out. But the information is always there; it doesn't disappear.

So, what if our feelings (which are in tune to our thoughts, and vice versa) are like wavelengths of electromagnetic radiation, and they are producing some sort of reaction (or reception) somewhere out there in the world? (The science associated with quantum physics points to a subatomic world that reacts and responds to waves of output generated through an intrinsic linking of our emotional life and mindset; with each and every one of us *as a causal agent.* I won't be going into this in depth, but it does raise fascinating questions and possibilities!)

If it is true that the energy we are sending out from our bodies can produce a reaction of some sort out in the world, then we want to deliberately craft those messages, mindful of the response we are seeking.

Do you turn on the television and press your thumb over the channel button for precisely five seconds and whatever program you land on at the end of that five seconds is the one you watch? Do you spin the radio dial (I know…most radios don't have "dials" anymore, but bear with me) and just listen to whatever station it lands on at the end of that spin? Of course not. You decide what you want, you select the precise channel that will give you what you want, and that's what you get.

What if everything is like that? What if we just don't know it? Or we don't believe it?

You see, it's important to believe it, because if you don't, you won't take advantage of the opportunities that are right in front of you. You've heard the old adage: "I'll believe it when I see it." But as I've just pointed out, there is a lot of information out there that we don't see. (The vast majority of the electromagnetic spectrum is entirely invisible). It is actually more appropriate to say: "I'll see it when I believe it."

If you are attempting to achieve something, but you deeply question your ability to actually achieve it, you may be prone to giving up too soon. And the reality may be that it isn't that the thing is impossible for you, it's just that you *believe* it is, and therefore you don't put as much effort into it as you would if you had absolute *faith* that you could achieve it.

Believe it, and then you will see it.

Once again, we are back to that confluence of vision, belief, and faith. In a practical sense, when we create a vision of something specific that we want in our lives, we've decided what we want to "see", just as we select a channel on TV.

You can be vague, of course. You can say, "I want something funny," and you could end up with a stand-up act by Dave Chappelle or you could end up watching Bridesmaids. Very different things, but both, arguably, funny. It really all depends on how much you want what you want (something funny) and how much you know just what you want (whether it's going to be Dave Chappelle or Bridesmaids).

Maybe you started thinking about your future a minute ago and you got worried that planning something too specific would cause you to miss out on something you might not even think of.

Could that happen?

Well, of course it could. But only in a very superficial sense.

When you set out to genuinely find and showcase your best self, you will draw into your sphere-of-being all the amazing things that support that ideal. You are not going to accidentally bypass what would have been your highest calling. If it's really your highest calling, you're not going to miss out on it by choosing the path to your best self. Assuming you are actively, consciously seeking to know who that is.

In a very concrete sense, you could imagine yourself walking down a road that splits into three different paths. You have a general sense of where you want to go, and you believe that the path farthest to the left from where you are standing is going to be your most direct route. But then you start wondering what you might encounter down the other paths, and you worry that you'll miss something by not choosing a different one. Wracked with indecision and fear of regret, you sit down at the fork in the road and cry.

Now, instead of leaving yourself open to the possibility of something better than what you've decided on, you just end up going nowhere. You are stalled out.

The great baseball manager (and player, and coach), Yogi Berra wrote a book titled, *When You Come to a Fork in the Road, Take It!* What he was saying is to trust your instinct. Don't ponder too long, and don't worry about going the wrong way.

Good heavens, if you start off down a path and you realize it's the wrong one, or not the best one, you can simply course correct. But if you refuse to take aim at anything in the first place because you fear that your aim will be off, chances are you will end up nowhere.

Goal number one: create a vision of what you want your life to look like.

You can begin doing this immediately.

A lot of refinement can be added as you go along but, for now, I want you to start creating mental images that hold at least some of the things you think you want in your life. It might be that you've never even done that before.

Would you like to go back to school and learn a trade?

Would you like to visit Roman ruins in Italy?

Would you like to earn a six-figure income?

Would you like to get married?

Would you like to live in the mountains? At the beach? In a valley next to a lake stocked with trout?

Don't be surprised if you immediately start editing your thoughts, or even shutting down certain parts. There may be a voice in your head that tells you that you are being greedy with your desires, or that you should be satisfied with what you have, or that it's selfish or even disrespectful toward God to imagine that *you* can create your own life. We think these thoughts even while, at the same time, championing and quoting things like William Ernest Henley's "I am the master of my fate; I am the captain of my soul."

Well, are you, or aren't you? What do you truly believe?

Ah! That "belief" thing again. You believe what you choose to believe, but if you would like to believe something other than what you believe now, then you have to start with a vision.

Say aloud to yourself something that you don't really believe right now. For example, "I am beautiful," or "I am capable of making a ton of money."

Now, what would you do if you believed it? If you were beautiful, for example. What clothes would you wear? How would you care for your appearance? What would you eat? Who would you allow yourself to approach and talk to? What kind of joy would you seek out? Here's the funny thing: it doesn't matter which came first—doing those things or believing you are beautiful. If you create a vision in your head of *you* as *beautiful,* and you say this to yourself, and you behave as if it were true, then your reality will begin to align with your vision.

Don't believe me? Try it out. Authentically, honestly, dutifully try it out. Not just once, after which you give up. You must hold to the vision.

Truly, if you create a vision, and you pull it into your consciousness again and again, and you focus on it, and dwell on it, and give your attention to it, you will come to believe it.

It happens all the time, even though you may not have been aware of it up to this point. If you see yourself as unattractive, or unintelligent, or bad at math, or incapable of art, or a loser, or fat, or slow, or poor, or unemployable, or any of a billion other things, then that is the belief you will create about yourself.

Conversely, if you change that vision—see yourself as brilliant, attractive, wealthy, gifted, talented, and so on—then *that* is what you will come to believe, and your belief will shape your reality. But you must *believe* before you can *become*. Once again, I have to reiterate: we are not believing what we see; *we are seeing what we believe.*

You might want to ask me, then: when I come to believe something different about myself, will that difference be literally manifested in my reality, or will it be my same reality, only now I see it differently?

The answer is this: *It will be literally manifested in your reality.*

CHAPTER FIVE

POSITIONING YOURSELF FOR SUCCESS

"The universe is not outside of you. Look inside yourself; everything that you want, you already are."

~Rumi

At some point in your evolution as a deliberate creator of your own life and destiny, you are going to go from taking charge of your internal world to actively taking charge of your external world.

How does this work?

Conceptually, it is this: *you will begin to live your life as if the person you wish to become is already who you are.*

There are some mental gymnastics involved here because the way you think about things now, in this exact moment, is not going to be the same as the way you will *come* to think about things when you are changing your life and pursuing your fondest dreams. Or when you have reached some of those milestones. And I'm going to ask you to put the cart before the horse—think the way you would think if you were already there. Behave the way you would behave if you were the sort of person you'd like to be.

Let's drill down on this.

Suppose you are envisioning yourself as a wealthy person, but your mentality reflects impoverishment. In other words, you believe, at a fundamental level, that there is only so much money to go around and you will: A) never get your share, and B) be stealing someone else's share if you do.

Further, you often suggest that successful people are "lucky;" you resent and disparage the rich, and you seek out the lowest prices on everything you buy regardless of relative quality or value. You may find yourself frequently complaining about the cost of things, or lamenting your inability to ever "get ahead," or blaming political processes or political parties for your economic situation.

You may feel a crippling inertia; the sense that you are powerless to fight the entities that determine the workings of the economy and the world. That they impact your life, but you don't seem to have any impact on *them*. So much of the world's resources are already going to the billionaires; how can there be any left for you? Your mentality and your behavior are self-reinforcing. You are tight-fisted with what you have because you are afraid there won't be any more. And you don't try to put yourself in a position to earn more because you think the system is fundamentally rigged toward keeping you down.

In some instances, a bit of soul-searching might even reveal that these are ways you mitigate your guilt over not taking control of and responsibility for your own life. And it works—from where you're standing, your circumstances look and feel real and true. If you are controlled by processes you can't change or even scarcely influence, then no one can hold you accountable for what you aren't able to do or become. You could very well be entirely convinced that these are the reasons your life does not look the way you would like it to.

Or, suppose you envision yourself as a full-time writer, but you don't practice the discipline to be even a *part-time* writer because you think that writing is something you need loads of time for, and if that isn't what your circumstances are providing you with right now, then you can't even get started.

I can promise you that if you accept any of the above, you have sabotaged your potential.

Live into your dream.

Align your thoughts and your actions with your desires.

If you want to be rich, you must think and speak as if abundance is possible in your life. You cannot resent rich people or blame anything outside yourself for causing your poverty. Similarly, you can't take the stance that what you have is more than enough and you should be happy with it. What are your struggles compared to someone who has even *greater* struggles? If you are telling yourself that you need to be content with what you have because to be otherwise would be *selfish* or *greedy*, let me just remind you to think of all the amazing good you could do and produce if you were truly, happily living up to your highest potential and realizing your own dreams.

If you want to be a writer, you must *write*—no matter what stands in your way. No self-limiting talk about how every story has already been told, and no one wants to hear what you have to say. Hard enough for *good* writers to sell books, let alone someone like *you*. Don't tell these things to yourself; they have no place in the picture you are creating. Just get your writing done. Yes, you *do* have time to write—when you prioritize your writing.

You must mold yourself in such a way that the structure of your perfect dream will be an exact fit to the person you have created of yourself. What would it take to do this?

Let's run through a scenario of what that could look like.

If, for example, you want the head management position where you work, you need to behave as if that is who you are.

Imagine how it would actually feel if you were serving in your new position; the deeper commitment, the greater responsibility. What would you be doing differently, what would your attitude be? Imagine yourself starring in this new role: confident, competent, a team player, a leader.

Envision yourself in this new job with all that goes with it: emotions, thoughts, actions, attitude.

If you are not already doing so, perform your job with increased conscientiousness. Up your game. (I would suggest this for anyone, in any position, as opportunity will open up to those who are actively ready for it). Repeat the mantra (which has been attributed to so many different people, I don't know where to give proper credit): "How I do anything is how I do everything"; make every effort to honor every responsibility; don't deceive yourself into thinking that "good enough" will pass muster.

Pay attention to how the job you are aiming for gets done. What skills are needed? What improvements could be made? What personal characteristics would make you a good fit? Listen to those above you. Learn everything you can about the organization: the challenges, the needs, and the opportunities.

Your actions are not just a reflection of your character, but also of your purpose, your drive, and your seriousness. Lift your consciousness from a mundane role to a place where you see the "big picture." Think in terms of the vision of your company or organization and begin to see yourself in a pivotal role.

There is a certain boldness of thought required of you to do this. When fear, or doubt, or insecurity step in (and they will), you must re-focus your thoughts on the goal and act in alignment with it—always.

Your mind is your biggest enemy and your greatest ally. You must train it to be fighting on the side of your highest self. As leadership expert Robin Sharma is fond of saying, "The mind is a wonderful servant, but a terrible master."

When you truly inhabit the place you want to be, and when you become the person you want to become *in your mind,* and if you hold faithfully to that vision, you cannot help but meet with success. The world will reorganize to fit your vision of it.

Most importantly, keep reminding yourself that your outer circumstances are less important than the vision of what you want. This vision will eventually re-order your circumstances according to the images and beliefs you are focused on in your mind, thereby changing your reality. In other words, it would be very easy to look around and say, "There is only one manager position and I know that person is never going to quit or be fired." This might cause you to base your dream on what you view as the reality, not on what you really want.

By the same token, it is not your role to facilitate the creation of a position by sabotaging someone else, or by generating false necessity for the organization. (Identifying real necessity and presenting it in a well-thought-out fashion that demonstrates increased value is a different matter).

You do not need to worry about how circumstances look on the outside. Your job is to let the Universe (or God, or Spirit, or consciousness, at large—whatever you want to call it) know what it is you desire, attach an emotion and a vision to that desire, and then act in concert with that vision *wherever you are right now.*

All the things that we can do to improve our circumstances are things that *must* be possible within the parameters of whatever already exists for us. Would you agree?

It would be pointless to tell you that, in order to change the way you visualize your existence, you need to move out of the ghetto you live in so that your brain can take in a new scenario. You might immediately shrug off any other suggestions and say, "Well, I can't do *that*, so never mind." And, rest assured, you don't need to. (You certainly *can* go to other neighborhoods and soak up the vibe and begin to get a feeling for what it's like to be somewhere else). You can begin to change your life *from* the ghetto, or *from* within the strained marriage, or *from* the dead-end job, or from any circumstances that seemingly govern your life right now.

We always begin where we are. There is no other way to do it.

Further, we must be willing to *act* as if our situation is different, even before it really *is* different. Or, at least, to act as if it is on the cusp of changing. Author Bryant McGill writes: "Every journey begins with the first step of articulating the intention, and then becoming the intention."

No matter what your desire is, taking action in your life to start moving in that direction is incredibly important. The magic doesn't usually happen in the initial actions, it happens when those actions, that belief, and that confidence *lead* you somewhere.

What you want to do (always!) is *position yourself for success.* What I mean by this is that no matter where you are right now; no matter whether you are just starting a journey to your ideal life, or you are well down the road, there are things you can do *now* to put you in a better position to jump into opportunities when they arise.

You don't start behaving like a promotable employee only when you find out that the position above you is about to become available. You do it from day one, so that when something better comes along, you are the first person the boss thinks of to fill that position. Or if you move to a different company or organization, those you worked with previously will be more than happy to recommend you to others. Because you have always behaved as if you are intending to go higher.

One of the best pieces of advice I was ever given while I was still a part-time professor and hoping for a full-time position was this: *act as if you are always on a job interview.* Another idea, along those same lines, that I learned when I was working for a pet store is: *act as if there is always a camera on you.*

Perform your job—all the time—as if someone is watching!

Because, guess what? They are.

In fact, I would take this a step further and suggest that you should monitor *all* your actions as if someone is watching. Not just your actions on the job. Be polite, help others, offer the respect and kindness you would want to receive from people.

Do you think you can be the person that is slow to perform your duties, who complains all the time, who talks trash about everyone, who thrives on drama, who indulges in "bad moods," who does the bare minimum to get by, who comes in late, who leaves early, who has an excuse for everything, who blames others—do you think you can be that person and *still* get a raise, a promotion, a pat on the back, or a stellar recommendation?

Everything you do, and say, and suggest by your actions is part of the package of *you*. If you are a barista at Starbucks, for example, your employer is noting way more than just whether or not you can make a good Frappuccino in a reasonable amount of time. They are noting everything about your work ethic, which includes your attitude, your character, your ability to get along with others, your willingness to learn new things, take on a challenge, or do the tough jobs. All of these things will influence them when they make a decision about whether to promote you, or how big of a raise to give you, or whether to keep you or let you go when times get tough.

If you take on the attitude that you are not going to do your best because you are not being paid enough, or treated fairly, or because no one notices anyway, or because it doesn't really matter, then you are running your game completely backwards. After all, you are the one who accepted the job in the first place. You applied for it, probably interviewed for it (and did your best to sound awesome), and you agreed to the wage or salary that was offered to you. Don't forget that you sold *your employer* a bill of goods, too. A bill of goods represented by the person that you are, and the work you are promising to do. You don't get to back out of all of that now that you have secured the position.

Your job is to do your best. Not because your company deserves it, but because *that's who you are*. That's where your integrity sits. The rest is none of your business. The rest is transitory. If you act in congruence with your vision, and your best intentions, and your ideal self, *regardless of what is going on around you*, you will eventually think, and behave, and envision yourself into a more appropriate, more fitting, more rewarding scenario.

And, by the way, just working hard and doing a good job doesn't automatically raise your station in life. The world is full of people who do that and still find themselves discontent or on a lower rung of the proverbial ladder than they had anticipated. The key is the *vision*, and being able to propel yourself toward it. You have to *know what you want*. You can't just work hard and hope something good comes your way, or that someone notices and hands you the keys to the kingdom. Maybe that will earn you a satisfactory day-to-day existence, or a good way to get the bills paid every month—*but is it everything you hoped your life would be?*

You must work with intention, on the right things, in the right direction, with unrelenting focus and faith.

You can't take on the attitude that what you want is impossible to achieve from where you're standing, and then walk around grumbling that life isn't fair and you've been dealt a bad hand of cards. Maybe you *have* been dealt a bad hand of cards, according to your view of such things, but there's still no one else but you who carries the responsibility of how that hand gets played.

Your only chance of increased peace, happiness, success, contentment—whatever it is that you're going for—is to actively choose and envision the life you want and do everything in your power to achieve it. You have to make the changes. Absolutely no one else can do it for you. *You are the responsible party.* Period.

Take any aspect of life, and this is the same method that can be used. If you are struggling to form successful romantic relationships—or any romantic relationship at all—you can't take the position that either A) you are undateable and no one wants you, or B) all the good men/women are taken. Both of these mindsets limit your opportunities and take the responsibility out of your hands, putting it on some sort of circumstance that you have no control over. Instead, you want to start with the vision (that is always the starting point)—the vision of *you* as someone desirable.

Have you ever deliberately envisioned yourself this way? You must do it. That person is there inside you. I promise you!

Try this: when you are getting yourself ready for the start of your day, imagine that *this* is the day you are going to meet someone special. How would that change how you put yourself together when you go into work? How would it change the things you say to everyone you encounter? How would it change the person you want to be *on this day*?

Everyone has things about them that are interesting, lovable, and desirable. *Own those things.* Pull your glorious, beautiful, unique authenticity out of that place you have buried it and put it on display for all the world to see. Your kindness, your hilarious wit, your grace under pressure, your strength, your patience, your humorous impatience, your flash, your style, your way with words, your sharp mind, your willingness to smile and laugh, your powers of perception, your sensitivity, your generosity, your courage. And so much more. The obvious things as well as the subtle things.

And, then, behave as if someone is watching. *That* someone.

When you encounter people who complain, criticize, or act poorly in other ways, do you find them attractive? Probably not. When you encounter someone who is being wholeheartedly and uniquely themselves, do you find them attractive? Well, of course you won't find *everyone* attractive who fits that description, but you would probably think of that person as an attractive person. A person that other people will find value in, and with whom they will want to spend time. You can be that person, too.

Focus on your assets, not on your faults. Put your best self on display. (Do it consciously, routinely, and habitually. This is the goal). Be kind and considerate. Be a person you would want to be around. *Be the kind of person someone would want to date.*

Yes, you have to be pleasant. To allow yourself to be critical, nasty, bitchy, grumpy, poopy—whatever word you might call it—is to indulge the addictions of your lower self. I call it indulgent because you are refusing to exercise normal, reasonable self-control. You are following the path of least resistance and giving in to your frustration, your impatience, your fear, and your insecurity. As if you are a child throwing a temper tantrum. You can do better. You can require more of yourself.

There is something inherently satisfying in taking the high road. You are not "sacrificing" your true feelings for the sake of being polite and gracious—you are setting and modeling higher standards, *and that feels good.* It also keeps you from swimming in the murky waters of regret when you let yourself say or do something that is not in alignment with who you really want to be. The outcome of your interactions may not always be what you desire (in other words, you can't control what happens with others, or how they respond, and it may not always be to your liking), but you can, at least, feel good about how you've handled your own part of the interaction.

The above does not mean having no boundaries. Maintaining civility and kindness in your interactions does not preclude you from disengaging with people who do not show the same respect, or who would use the other person's kindness as a tool of manipulation. You can have clear expectations about what you will and will not tolerate in interactions, but if you allow yourself to become rude and unpleasant, you are, in effect, polluting the energy around you. Everyone feels it, and no one is served by it. Least of all you.

This is what it means to position yourself for success. In the workplace, and in your personal life.

Sure, you may not be able to jump right away into that thing that you really want to do—you may not be able to start the business, or buy the property, or change jobs, or get married, or get into Harvard just as soon as you form the idea that that's what you would like to do. But you *can* begin to lay the groundwork. You can research, practice, save money, meditate, get fit, lose weight, write every day, teach yourself discipline, teach yourself patience, learn a new language, if that will help. The point is: there is *always* something you can do right now that will help position you so that when opportunity presents itself, you need only step into it.

This way of thinking is effective in virtually every part of your life. Try these things:

If you want new clothes, clean out your closet. Throw away anything that has outlived its constitutional integrity (meaning, it has holes, stains, or is misshapen with age and use); donate anything that you don't use or that doesn't look great on you. Use the clothing you have left to creatively, conscientiously put yourself together in a presentable fashion each day. The deliberation with which you consider your "look," and the unloading of the items that no longer serve you will make you feel good and it will create space—physically and *meta*physically—for new things to replace what you have relinquished.

If you want a new house, or to change locations, clean the one you have. Again, getting rid of stuff you don't need or don't use—the exact steps you would have to take if, for example, your move was imminent. Do it in advance and watch what happens. In the meantime, you will enjoy a cleaner, less-chaotic environment. Rearrange the furniture. Hang some pictures you love. Light some candles. Clean your windows. Play some awesome music. Make the most of the place you've got. (For some epic inspiration, read Marie Kondo's book, *The Life Changing Magic of Tidying Up*). In addition, feel free to go online and look at homes for sale. This will offer great inspiration for creating images in your mind of the kind of house and location you ultimately want to live in.

If you want to make more money, behave more responsibly with what you have. If you think to yourself: "I'm going to start a savings account just as soon as I get my next raise," you are already behind the train. Start saving now. It doesn't have to be much. $5 a week. Make a budget. Use it. But don't get stingy—literally or energetically. Don't adopt a "cheap" mentality—where you forget that there are a hell of a lot of things for which it's worth paying some extra money. Abundance is real. Abundance is ready for the taking. As soon as you respect and value both money and the things it can buy.

Watch what happens.

When you are focused on getting better—in all areas of your life— you will find that you are no longer so interested in thinking about what's wrong, or bad, or unfair. You will be too busy *changing your life*. You will wonder why you hadn't done it before. You will wonder why more people aren't doing it, too. You may even start to help others turn their lives around.

What you focus on expands. It is accentuated and intensified. I said it earlier in this book. So, make a point to focus on what you *want*, not on what you *don't* want. Complaining, or griping, or criticizing are useless in their own way, but they also draw attention from a mindset and thought patterns that can actually make things better. They allow you to wallow in energy that saps rather than invigorates. Don't indulge in that crap. Train your mind. Discipline your thoughts.

And as you are doing your work, you will find your world changing; the horizon of your potential broadening as your estimation of your own capabilities undergoes a re-set or a re-wiring. You will be inhabiting a place in your reality that once only existed in your vision.

And when that happens, you will have succeeded. You'll have an understanding of creating from limitless possibilities *at an experiential level*. Because you will have become that person who is capable of that achievement. And you will understand what it takes to develop the parts of yourself that move you forward, and the more you develop those parts, the more you grow—and your potential keeps morphing and expanding.

You get what you want by becoming a person who is willing and able to create it.

And most of us don't start out being that person; it's what we get to by walking this path. So, when you look at where you want to be, you have to really think about what kind of person you need to become in order to get there. I think we have a sense of this automatically. Or, rather, we know that at the beginning of our journey that we are *not* that person. This can be discouraging because we are not seeing the stepping-stones that lead us from where we are to where we need to be—we are just seeing the gulf; the difference in those two realities.

But all you're really required to do at that point is *take the next step.*

Identify what the next action is and take it. You don't have to become a different person all at once. You just have to be willing to walk out on the path that will lead you there. One step; then the next; then the next. Often, each step gives you the tools, and skills, and confidence to move to the next one. But you won't know that by cowering down on the pathway and refusing to move because the vision in the distance scares you.

Do you believe you can influence your own destiny? Do you believe that, to a great extent, you are responsible for what your life looks like? These are important questions.

If we believe we are responsible for the choices that shape our lives, then why would we put so much emphasis on the *circumstances* of our lives?

Are they not changeable, then? Are we beholden to these circumstances; victims of someone else's choices or of "the way things are"?

Either we are responsible for our lives, or we are not. Consider this when you are blaming circumstances outside your control for the life-situation you find yourself in. If those circumstances determine your life, then why bother with anything? It is a bit like believing in predestination, isn't it?

But if you can believe that no matter what events show up in your life (whether you chose them, or they just happened to you), that you have *agency* and *responsibility* in how you respond and what comes of these things, then you gain a sense of internal power, and ownership over your own life. You begin to feel that even though life may try to wrest the steering wheel from your grasp, you do not have to throw up your hands in defeat. There is always a choice about how you are going to show up in those circumstances, and who you are going to be. This is ultimate power.

We are all creators! If we embrace the notion that we are here to live creatively and to master this task/talent/gift to the greatest extent possible, we will live our lives from that assumption, that starting point. We will then manifest a very different reality than one in which we did not perceive ourselves as part of the creative process.

You get to create your own life!

What if you believe that? Then it follows that you have to take responsibility for it. *If you don't like your life, create a different one.*

CHAPTER SIX

EMBRACE THE STRUGGLE

"Those tasks that have been entrusted to us are difficult; almost everything serious is difficult; and everything is serious."

~Rainer Maria Rilke

In the previous chapters, my aim has been to lay down some groundwork—placing an emphasis on the importance of thought, vision, belief, and mindset regarding the form one's life ultimately takes. With that understanding in place, it becomes clear that you are more in control of your life than you might have previously imagined. And if you have at least *some* control of your life (I would argue that you have a *lot*), you need to take the steering wheel out of the hands of fate and put it back into your own hands. You need to start deliberately steering your life.

Imagine such a thing! Deciding where you want your life to go, *and then going there.*

And, sure, you don't have to. You can drift along and see where you end up. It's your own choice, after all. But maybe you can also acknowledge that if it's *possible* to chart your course and choose your own destiny, it's hard not to be fascinated by that idea. When you can inject as much meaning as you are capable of into this riotous merry-go-round of life, I would argue that it's a bit boring not to. You can be a force of change, and progress, and purpose in your life. *By choice.* Do you see? How incredible such an idea is? Won't that kind of life mean more to you than one you acquired by default?

Assuming you *do* want to give this a go, the following list is a set of the "must do's" to get you on the path toward the life of your dreams:

- Decide on a destination.

- Chart a path toward that destination. (Course-correcting allowed).

- Consider *who* you need to be to complete this path and start becoming that person.

- Take steps—even small ones—along that path every day.

That's the basic formula. That's you, *in the driver's seat.*

What is it that you want? To become an architect? A horse trainer? A college graduate? A political activist? Do you want to start a business? Make more money? Be more fulfilled? Get fit? Maybe write a book, run a marathon, take up painting, hone your psychic skills. (Hey, it could be anything!)

You have to be conscious and deliberate with your choices but, as discussed before, they don't have to be the "right" choices or your final choices. The idea is to get in the habit of making choices about what you do and what happens to you, rather than letting your life run on autopilot (which is what most people do).

Spend some time really thinking about the possibilities at the forefront of your mind and then make a choice that feels right for the moment. From there, chart a path toward the destination you've selected and start walking on that path. One step at a time, over and over. As my dad was fond of saying on long hikes: "Just keep putting one foot in front of the other."

I can't stress how critical it is to *just take the next step.* So very often we become paralyzed because of the obstacles that lurk *down the road.* We know we will have to face something we fear, or something we're not good at, or something that causes us anxiety, or something that we know nothing about.

No question about it; we are right about those things. They will cross our path. They will set up roadblocks on our highway.

But not yet. And, right now, you don't have to worry about those things. You just have to worry about the very next step. Just that one. Figure out what it is and take it.

Now, figure out the next one.

Take it.

Along the way, you will learn more about yourself and about your interests, and your ultimate goals will evolve accordingly. You will also gain confidence, and you will realize that it *is* possible to persevere on a course of action, even if it's scary and fraught with uncertainty. As you persist in walking forward—tremble as you might, with each step—you will gain the tools, skills, and resources to break through the obstacles that inevitably present themselves. This always happens—so long as you do not give up— and you will see a beautiful symmetry begin to emerge from the chaos.

Probably the biggest takeaway from my last couple of years of getting very specific about what kind of life I want, and setting goals, and pursuing the things that are most important, compelling, and meaningful to me is this: I have come to know myself better.

With that knowledge comes increased self-love, self-trust, and self-care.

And from that place, all the other stuff becomes more accessible: the resilience, the perseverance, the dedication, determination, and discipline.

And the self-knowledge grows yet again; my horizons and the edge of my perceived limitations expand outward. It's a wondrous feedback loop.

It's quite possible, though, that your self-knowledge is not at that place yet, so don't panic. If nothing comes to mind as a goal or a first step, you can use the backtracking method. You could take a few moments to imagine what you would like your life to look like—5, or 10, or even 20 years from now. Where do you want to live? How much money do you want to be making? What kind of life do you see yourself inhabiting? Who do you see yourself being? (Think about your values). What are the activities you would do? What are the things and people and events you would surround yourself with? What is important for you to have in your life? Get the big picture ideas as clear as possible and see if that points you in the direction of some of the possible ways you might get there.

Creating the life of your dreams isn't about just getting to this physical place where you have all the "things" and circumstances you want to have; that's called winning the lottery.

Instead, it's about creating a life that is deeply meaningful to you, so that those outer circumstances are, in many ways, a reflection of who you become and what you hold dear. You want to have what you have because you did what it took to get there. And, by extension, when you do what it takes to "get there," you will absolutely have everything that you want. It is a lovely, magical equation.

But what I also want to point out is that if you choose nothing, and if you do nothing, the place you end up will be a paler, diminished version of where you *could have been.* Period. Even if you win the lottery. And wherever you're at, the only way to get to a place that's better is to move in that direction—even if it is only in tiny increments.

Problematically, the things we are required or obligated to do, like going to work so we can earn a paycheck in order to get food, clothing, and shelter are *not* usually the things that are the most important to us for our ultimate happiness, or for us to be able to say we're living the life we want. But they *are* the most urgent things, and the things that, if we stop doing them, will cause immediate and significant consequences.

This is one of the main reasons why more people don't move forward on chasing their dreams once they've got bills to pay. Paying the bills takes so much time and effort. Not to mention everything else that comes along with being an independent adult: making meals; doing laundry; maintaining the house; taking care of children, or pets, or parents. How on earth will you find the time or energy to do anything else?

Besides, there *is* a certain satisfaction in doing these tasks. There can be fulfillment in being a good worker, a good parent, and a responsible, independent adult. Getting those bills paid, providing for a family, and every so often going to Disneyland, or a ball game, or out camping. It's very easy to get lulled into the comfort of a predictable, manageable, *functional* life.

Maybe this even adds to the problem. We may not be living our *best* life, and we may not be moving forward as fast or as far as we once dreamed, but it's not so bad, is it? It is this exact conundrum that causes most people to throw up their hands and conclude that a better life is simply not possible; that the dreams they dreamed as a child did not take into consideration the obligations and responsibilities of being an adult.

Then, too, there is an idea that arises out of this normalcy; this functionality; this generalized satisfaction: maybe this is as good as it gets. Maybe this is all there is. After all, we don't really *know*, do we? We've only got the one life. We can't make comparisons against a previous life wherein we went for bigger, grander goals and found that life could be more fulfilling. Is there more joy waiting around the corner? Could we live our lives differently? It might be very easy to say that we'll just never know, and maybe it's better to enjoy our simple satisfactions than to go chasing the pot of gold at the end of the rainbow, and potentially running amok.

By the time we've given any thought to it, it's time to go to work again, or cook dinner, or placate a bored child, or put together an overdue report. Best to just focus on what movie we'll get to go see this weekend than worry about changing our whole life and upsetting the apple cart.

These obligatory things—and the attendant resignation to how much of our time and life-force they will command—are also one of the main reasons we stop listening to our inner voice that tells us who we are and what we could be. And that's a shame. That inner voice should never be allowed to fall silent. It is like our inner compass; our mechanism for course-corrections. And if you are one of those people who still feels that tug on your soul—that sensation that there is something more to your life, and you're missing out on it—then tuning in is even more crucial.

I'm here to tell you that your dreams are all still very possible and that it's time you woke up to that possibility. You are capable of more. There *is* greater potential in your life. It isn't just a myth. And if you are one of those people who have a sense of this in your gut, then this is for you.

Yes, despite how little money you think you make; despite how many tasks vie for your time and effort; despite how high your taxes are; despite what state you live in, who the president is, or what job you currently have. Or even if you don't have any job at all.

In *most* cases, it is a person's belief and effort that gets them where they want to go. And the rest just shifts the timeline and, sometimes, the level of effort required. But there is virtually nothing that qualifies as a permanent barrier to your success unless you believe it and give up.

But you must be deliberate about your dreams, your choices, and your intentions—every step of the way. And you're going to have to make some sacrifices. You have to prioritize the things that don't *seem* to matter over things that always feel urgent. Because the former will get you where you want to go, and the latter will keep you stuck. You have to push yourself forward in the direction of your dreams—however hard it is, however long it takes—if they really matter to you.

And this is often where people bog down. It's fairly easy to practice a "way of being" for several days or weeks—or as long as the inspiration lasts (more on that later)—but profound and lasting changes to habits and thought processes take place over months and years. And that's if you don't give up.

This process is very important, though, and by fortifying yourself mentally and learning some skills that I'm going to share with you, you can persevere. And perseverance is a game changer. It's the boots-on-the-ground kind of grind that allows you to discover who you are, what you're made of, and how to let your inherent light shine brilliantly. It changes everything. It makes all your work *count* for something.

Think about this: the lithospheric plates that the continents and ocean basins are situated on move, on average, about 1 to 2 inches per year, which seems incredibly insignificant. But over vast periods of geologic time, that movement has shaped and re-shaped the earth's surface in dramatic and profound ways. Entire continents have come together and split apart again. Mountains have risen miles into the sky and then eroded, stone by stone, to mere hills. So it is with us: the small changes can result in huge and lasting impacts in our lives.

Move forward on your goals. Every day if you can. Even if it's only a tiny bit. When a year goes by, that tiny bit of daily movement will have added up to significant change. And something else will happen; something magical. You will have momentum on your side. You will have a full year of taking action, and this action will inspire you and heighten your confidence to take even more action.

A feedback loop is created. As you think about your dream, and you plan your course, and you practice living in integrity with your values, your own self-love and self-respect will grow. You will have more clarity, and that clarity will fuel more action, and that action will bring rewards, and the fact that you—YOU—are the machine that runs your life will be visible and satisfying. But whatever you feel stands in your way, you still must begin. You have to take a step forward, and then take another.

There is no way around this, and no excuse meaningful enough to justify trying to elude it.

No, fear is not an excuse. Fear is an obstacle that you must overcome.

If you need to earn a degree to get the job you want, then apply at colleges, register for classes, and start going. Even if you can only take one class per semester. Many people start out this way. *I started out this way.* Do not let yourself be deterred because you are 40, or 60, or 90 years old. You are *not* the only "older" student to ever start college. I happen to know. And older students are often the best.

If you want to become a writer and you don't believe you have time to write, just write for 5 minutes a day, consistently, every day. There is no one that *can't* do that. Write crap, if you must, but *write.* You will develop a habit. You will build confidence. You will get better. And you will also have a head start on your goals that you won't want to relinquish. It will push you to keep at it.

If you have a business and you want that business to do better, it is important that you identify the areas in which it is floundering, consider the actions that will boost it (even if you can't take those actions right away, or even if you don't know how that will look for your particular company), and then start putting something in place to get there. You can't put your head in the sand and blame your struggle on the economy, or your marketing director (although you might need to find another one), or the price of tea in China. There may be multiple reasons, but they don't negate the fact that if something is going to change, the impetus must come from you, irrespective of any outer circumstances. Think in terms of taking *absolute responsibility* for achieving the results you want.

You have to *see* where you want your business to go, and what you want it to look like. You must be able to imagine something better, so you know where to direct your aim. It is easy to avoid this step, saying that the future is hard to see, that solutions can be murky. And, indeed, this is the very thing that may be stopping you. How can you do something *when you have no idea what to do?* Or you have a sense of what you need to do, but don't know how to start. Or you're *afraid* to start. Or you're just too damn busy to start.

But we can learn that we are only seemingly stymied. Doing nothing will not buy you time. It will buy you heartache. It will buy you regret.

Now, find your courage and wipe that mirror or window clean. Yes, this is a moment for brave and bold action. Take a good, hard look. Outside or inside. What needs to happen?

Still don't know? Then, that's your first step.

Dissect the pieces of your business, or your dream, or your ideal self. Journal about it. Write down your realizations, your concerns, your next set of questions. Then visualize what a perfect business looks like—*as far as you know*. Fantasize about it, for God's sake. Those images you produce in your mind are part of the creative process. They are like an investment that eventually yields much bigger, more meaningful, more concrete returns.

And this introspection will also tune your attention to your authentic self; your inner voice; your own supreme clarity.

Here's the thing: those interlocking gears I mentioned earlier of Belief, Faith, and Vision run up against some other interlocking gears: Mindset, Thoughts, Goals, and Action. None of these things, alone, is a magic bullet that puts your life on track. But, by the same token, we often can't manage more than one when we are first learning. Eventually, we come to understand how to practice all of them, and how each of them can reinforce the other.

Let me give you a sense of what this looks like, taking one piece at a time.

1. **Choose a mindset.** Like: "I have the ability to get where I want to be." "I can learn new skills." "I can seek help when I need it." "I can get better." "I can practice my craft." "I don't have to be a prisoner to my past." The key here is to embrace a mindset that gives you *choice, responsibility*, and *empowerment.*

(CHOICE. RESPONSIBILITY. EMPOWERMENT. Write those words down somewhere. Think about your relationship with them).

2. **Train your thoughts to be supportive of your desired mindset.** This means *not* indulging in negative thought patterns such as, "This is never going to work. I'm not smart enough, strong enough, disciplined enough," etc. (These patterns are frighteningly easy to fall into because many people—maybe even *most* people— have default thought patterns dominated by habits of negative thinking). Going back to the example of math; instead of saying, "I am not good at math," the appropriate supportive thought pattern of a mindset that believes getting better is totally possible would be, "I am not good at math….*yet.*" Or, "I am getting better at (fill in the blank) every day." Or even a very simple mantra like the one I used when I was teaching a summer class and writing a book: "I can do this!"

3. **Set goals that bring you closer to your ideal life and your ideal self.** This requires you to sit down and actually set those goals. Write them down. Make them a concrete reality. Goals that can't even take form on paper have little to no chance of taking form anywhere else. The kinds of goals I'm talking about are not a things-to-do list. They will not be: finish the laundry; buy groceries; work on the report that is due on Monday. They will be things like:

- Research the application process at my local community college.

- Write 1,000 words a day

- Find a Toastmasters group so I can get better at public speaking

- Apply to 5 jobs this week. (Or 6, or 10, or 20).

- Open a savings account and decide on a $ goal for each month.

- Practice kindness this week. You can add more specificity by stating exactly how this will happen (i.e. "I will not let social media posts trigger me to say mean things," or "I will compliment at least 4 people this week").

- Purchase some starter pots and seeds for my summer garden.

There are countless examples I could offer. Obviously, you will tailor *yours* to suit your "big picture" goals. The main point being: these are things you are not *required* to do, but they are steps along a path that will bring you closer to a place you would ultimately like to be.

#4. Train your thoughts to be supportive of your goals. (Which you can now do because you have trained yourself to have the right mindset). This is similar to #2, but it is specific to the goals you have set in #3. In my office I have a quote taped to the side of my file cabinet right near my desk. It's something Steven Pressfield said in his book, *The War of Art*. It reads: "If you can just keep those huskies mushing, sooner or later the sled will pull in to Nome." This is what I'm talking about. I can't indulge in thoughts about how crappy my book is turning out, or that it will never be finished, or that I'm never going to be "good enough." All I've got to do is "keep those huskies mushing." That's my job. That's the action I take—putting one foot in front of the other—and that's where I keep my focus.

#5. Take action (even if the action is somewhat small) every single day toward your goals. You've made your list of goals in #3—*now do those things!* Arrrgh! This is where the inertia is going to feel almost overwhelming (and I'll talk about that in a moment). But keep checking your mindset, keep checking your thoughts, keep putting those internal things in place and you *will* be able to support the external action. When you do it, you will feel amazing. Your confidence will soar.

This is truly where the magic happens. When you consistently move in the direction of self-improvement, you literally change who you are. ***When you change who you are, you change the possibilities of what can happen to you and for you.*** The world broadens along with your vision. You gain access to things, people, ideas, money, potential, opportunity that you couldn't have even imagined before.

You also stop being manipulated by the negativity, the drama, and the sensationalism that dominates our society and our media. You learn to shut that crap out and guard your psyche. *You* are the one who determines your mindset, your thoughts, and your potential. Not the president. Not the economy. Not the war in Syria, or the wall in Mexico, or the murder rate in Detroit. Choose your thoughts; make them good, and guard them like precious gold.

The hardest thing to do is to just get started. It sounds so simple—and it *is* simple—but every day we automatically come up with a rationale for why we can't do what we know we need to do. Or, worse, why we can't do it *right now*. Like the fact that we are already so busy with our current obligations it seems laughable to think of adding anything more. We tell ourselves that we'll start the work required to get our lives on track *just as soon as things settle down*. As soon as we're less busy. As soon as the divorce is finalized. As soon as we finish school. As soon as we get a different job. The list is inexhaustible.

And I say this is *worse* because we placate ourselves by insisting that *we will still do it*—just not yet. If we said we weren't going to do it at all, we'd have to deal with that. We'd have to come to terms with our rationalization. But if we just put it off, we get a pass.

The reason it's hard to start something is because of inertia—the tendency to resist a force that will cause a change in our current state.

To illustrate this, imagine two guys riding around in an old VW Beatle that suddenly breaks down in the middle of the road. The driver cranks the key: once, twice, three times. He moves the gears around, hoping for a random miracle, but nothing happens. Horns are blaring behind the two men in the car. They know they need to move the car out of the road. So, they get out and start pushing. At first, the car doesn't move. The two guys step back, stretch out, re-grip, take a different foothold, and throw themselves into it again. Finally, they get it rolling. They know—intuitively and from experience—that this is the critical moment. They can't let up on the pressure or they'll be back to square one. Even though their muscles are straining, and their feet are slipping, they just keep pushing. Within a few moments, the car is rolling easily, and it takes very little effort to push it the rest of the way off the road.

Momentum.

But to get to momentum, you have to overcome inertia, and that's the hard part.

In his book just referenced, *The War of Art*, Steven Pressfield writes: "Resistance cannot be seen, touched, heard, or smelled. But it can be felt. We experience it as an energy field radiating from a work-in-potential. It's a repelling force. It's negative. Its aim is to shove us away, distract us, prevent us from doing our work."

He adds later in another section that, "...its target is the epicenter of our being: our genius, our soul, the unique and priceless gift we were put on earth to give and that no one else has but us."

Think about that. You are not overcoming inertia or resistance just to get a better job, or a better relationship, or more money, or a vacation (though these could all be part of the overall package); you are overcoming it to get to the very reason you exist; the very essence of your humanity and reason-for-being. What you *could* be is your greatest self, but just as with anything of tremendous value, getting to that self is not easy.

Think about the ways this inertia or resistance bog you down. It's not just the busy schedule I mentioned earlier. That might be hard to overcome, but nowhere near as difficult as, say, releasing the emotional strings that hold a person in a codependent relationship with their spouse. Maybe we feel criticized, unsupported, controlled; we're suffering and we feel we lack choice.

But just because this conflict and feeling of imprisonment exists in someone's life does not mean that they are incapable of improving, changing, or even escaping, if need be. What is imperative is recognizing and acknowledging the state of our emotional life as well as taking responsibility for the trade-offs we're accepting. Let's just be clear with ourselves: why are we where we are? Is this what we want?

To be our best selves, we must master our weaknesses. There's an *overcoming* that must take place. This implies a struggle, true enough. But implicit in the idea of struggle is the idea that the struggle yields something. Not just the *result* of the struggle (the win, the achievement, the forward movement, the break from a dependency, or addiction, or whatever), but the struggle *itself*.

There is something enlightening and enlivening and fulfilling about doing the hard work and seeing it pay off. Whatever our talents are, they are not nearly what they could be with greater effort, finer polish, and deeper refinement. Is it not worth getting to that part of ourselves; that part of our ultimate potential?

The famous racehorse, Seabiscuit, didn't just walk out of his stall one day and trounce War Admiral in a match race. He had to be trained up to it; his talents had to be shaped; his mind had to be readied; his instincts and his physical prowess required sharpening. We are no different. We may be small, and knobby-kneed, and lacking in flash (like Seabiscuit), but it doesn't mean we don't have something brilliant to offer.

When you start with the basics: have a vision, set some goals, be accountable, and work your ass off, you are learning an abundance of information about yourself; and you are learning what you ultimately find meaningful, and how to value it. We value the things we have to struggle for; or pay a lot for; or which are rare and, therefore, precious. I think we have an innate desire to *earn* things. Because this allows us to gain competence, and when we gain competence, we gain confidence, and confidence feels good and is good for us. You don't have to teach a child to feel proud of itself when it accomplishes a task at which it has worked hard. The child feels it automatically. This means it is evolutionarily and biologically a good way to feel—under the circumstances of having accomplished something worthwhile, anyway.

(On a side note, the feeling of being "proud" of one's particular ethnicity or nationality is not the same feeling. There is no need to accomplish anything for that "pride" to happen. And I would suggest that calling it "pride" is not even appropriate. It is more a feeling of reverence for one's roots and heritage. A happy embracing, perhaps. Not pride, though, and I think this distinction is important for the point I'm trying to make about what causes this feeling, and why we are wired to have it).

We don't necessarily *know* what is meaningful to us when we just drift through life. But when we have fought, and struggled, and tried, and helped, and been helped, and asked, and cried, and worked, and failed, and learned, we "come into our own". We learn who we really are, and sometimes that means that what we thought was important to us when we were younger—or just less experienced—simply falls away.

But sometimes the things that were important to us *remain* important to us—especially if we have come to recognize them as a sincere and honest reflection of our natural proclivities and sensibilities. Those interests or talents or preferences that point to who we are: our uniqueness as a person, and even the special ways we can connect with other people or touch their lives in important ways. And this illuminates for us the fact that our talents are this unbelievably precious and priceless gift which we come to realize must be shared.

So that, eventually, all this goal-setting, and planning, and working, and persevering, and being disciplined, and sacrificing, and faltering, and trying again—all this that we *thought* was so we could have this great life that we've dreamed of—becomes more about evolving into a more conscious and conscientious human being. And then we reach a place where we are able to offer to the world our experience, our gifts, and our talents, and the great life is just a by-product of all that. We enjoy it, but it's not why our life has meaning.

We think about our future, we dream about what we want to do, and be, and have, not just because there is a certain way of life that we want to attain. What we come to realize is that there is also a certain way of *being* that we want to attain—and we could call this our highest self. Even those who are content with their position or status or accomplishments in life might still wonder if they are acting as their highest self.

Or they may have never even thought about it. But I think most of us have. Perhaps not in those exact terms, but in some form or another we wonder who or what we could be if we brought our greatest talents and deepest courage to bear in some part (or many parts) of our lives. I guess we could call these things our "highest values," and if we lived in accordance with them every day of our lives, we would be living a life of deep responsibility, personal choice, and ultimate freedom and meaning.

The trouble is, when we start to walk down that path, we realize that it's difficult. It entails discomfort, potential failure, the pain of effort (and sometimes of rejection or humiliation, or just the physical pain of pushing yourself farther than you ever have), sacrifice, uncertainty, even the loss of friends and family who might not support what you're doing or understand why you're so "driven" to do it. They will tell you to rest; to relax more; to get off your high horse.

And then impatience comes along. There's no big breakthrough. You will start to wonder how long you should persist, or if your persistence will ever pay off. You're busting your ass, day after day, and nothing seems to be happening. You will experience stretches of sameness. You may not like it, but this is all part of the process.

So why bother?

To find out all that you have to offer when you demonstrate courage, exhibit grit, and persevere. To test your limits in this life you've been blessed with. To touch the sky, and plumb the depths, and really know the answer to the questions: *"Who am I? And what can I do with all I have been given?"*

CHAPTER SEVEN

ENVISIONING AND GOAL SETTING

"We are limited not by our abilities but by our vision"

~Anonymous

At this point, you are probably recognizing how important it is to reinforce your vision of yourself and your ideal life with a specific mindset, positive and creative thoughts, and meaningful actions that either help you achieve certain, tangible goals or develop your character into someone who can. But what has not been addressed explicitly is how you create that vision in the first place.

How do you know what to envision? How do you know who or what you want to be? How do you know what you want your life to look like? For some of you, these may seem like strange questions, but for many, they are all too real.

Why do you think so few people ever make big changes in their lives?

Why do you think that a person who has always held mediocre jobs will continue to hold mediocre jobs, year after year?

It isn't because that person is *fundamentally* mediocre and lacks the potential to move up in the world. It isn't because their circumstances have hemmed them in (though they may believe this). It isn't because they didn't get a degree, or because they got one in the "wrong" field.

Almost always it is because they have never allowed themselves to envision anything better—perhaps because they never thought of it, or they don't know how, or they just didn't believe it was possible. They have literally shaped their reality around their perception of themselves and their abilities. (Which is what we all do, by the way, for better or worse).

Here's a challenge: go on whatever social media platform you prefer and post the following question: "What goals have you set for this year?"

Chances are, very few of your friends have bothered to set goals. Maybe you haven't, either. Maybe they will think some up in order to be able to answer that question that you've posted (and you can consider yourself to have done them a favor); maybe they will mention a few standard ones ("I want to lose 10 pounds," "I want to eat more healthy," "I want to get a better job."); maybe they simply won't answer the question at all.

Or maybe—as I've been seeing lately—they won't find it as fun an exercise as you had hoped! It seems almost as if there is a "counter" movement to the very *idea* of setting goals. You might be viewed as sanctimonious—if not an outright bully—by encouraging one and all to try it on. If this happens for you, it's just another chance to stay focused on what you're trying to accomplish. At the end of the day, it's just a fun idea, something on your mind…let it be. And there just may be many who give it some thought and *that* lines up with your intention.

Remember this: it is often the case that when you try to improve yourself, others recognize their own lack of will or desire, and resent you for yours. They will try to deflect their own embarrassment onto you, so that instead of deeply engaging with their own angst around the subject, they will try to make *you* feel bad for being proactive about your life.

Here's the problem, though, of *not* setting goals and creating a vision: *if you don't know where you're going, you're never going to get there.* You have to think about where you want to go (in terms of what you want from your year, and from your life), and you have to set some goals to get you there.

Last year, one of my goals was to walk 35 miles per week, which would amount to a total of 1,820 miles for the year. I used my Fitbit to track my steps, and I religiously logged my totals on a daily and weekly basis. Sometimes I was over, sometimes I was under, but I just kept carrying those totals through, week after week. After the year was over, I had walked 1,821.6 miles—a scant 1.6 miles over my goal. Could I have pushed myself more than that? Was 35 miles per week literally my limit, and that's why I barely went over it?

The reality is, if we set a goal with the intention of achieving it, and we put the right supports in place, we will probably achieve it. We will achieve *that* specific goal. Without the goal, my totals would have been *far* less—probably by hundreds of miles. I would not have been nearly as motivated to get those steps in.

But what you can see is that the goal also put a ceiling on what I was going to accomplish.

The first problem is that most people don't take aim at anything at all. The second problem is that when they do, they aim too low. (It is possible to aim too high, but those that are taking the process seriously usually don't). So, how do you get it right?

While writing this book, I used a variety of techniques to keep myself writing every day: sometimes I would say that I was going to log a certain number of hours for the week (daily count didn't matter as long as the weekly count was on target). Then I tried writing every day but limiting the time, so I didn't feel overwhelmed by the obligation. Then I settled on writing 1,000 words a day (this was during my winter break when I wasn't teaching classes), which caused me to question why I wasn't writing 2,000 a day instead. Finally, I asked the most important question of all: *What am I trying to accomplish?*

Turns out, I knew the answer to that question because I had already figured that out in my planning phase for this project. (This would be the "charting a path toward the destination" part that I mentioned in the previous chapter). I had decided that I wanted the book done by early

February. All right, then, if a completed manuscript (for this type of book) runs somewhere between 40,000 and 50,000 words, then how many words did I need to write every day to make my goal? Given what I had already written, and the time I had left, 1,000 words a day was adequate.

Of course, that doesn't tell the whole story. Because writing this book is not my only obligation. I am also doing the final re-writes on my previous book, figuring out the publishing and marketing strategy for that one, making time to drive with my oldest son who is trying to get his license, planning and prepping for my next semester of classes, and still getting those 35 miles in.

Given these other things that I know I am going to be doing, it doesn't make sense to simply set my goal at 1,000 words a day and cross my fingers that I can *always* achieve that. So, this week I'm setting my goal at 2,000 a day so that I can create some buffer during a slow week for when things get a little more hectic. (Once the next semester starts, my word count for whatever I'm working on at that time will probably drop to 300 or 500, but that's OK because I'll be teaching, and that will be my primary focus. But I won't *stop* writing).

The vision for your life is a bit like my "What am I trying to accomplish?" question. You've got to see the big picture so that you can strategically line up your goals to support that vision. But if you don't have that big picture in place, you're like a lost hiker without a compass. You don't know where to point your efforts. You don't know what your efforts should yield. In that scenario, the default position is almost always to just drift wherever life takes you. And in the absence of steering and a target, you will likely drift somewhere less meaningful. In some cases, people drift right into hopelessness and depression.

What I want to help you out with in this chapter is how to know what vision to create for your life if this is something you've never done, or never even thought about before.

There are two pieces of this "vision" puzzle to look at as you are thinking about how to start living your life with deliberation and choosing your own path. These are:

1. **Where you want to go and what you want to do.** This piece is going to include things like your dream job, your financial situation, what sort of place you would like to live in, what kinds of things you would like to spend your time doing. It would be impossible to suggest all the things you could think about here, but consider hobbies, relationships, travel, practices, pastimes, family, education, and so on.

2. **Who you want to become.** If you could grant yourself the personality traits that you find most desirable, what would they be? How do you want to see yourself next year? In ten years? What adjectives come to mind? Courageous, committed, disciplined, daring, patient, relaxed, strong, respected, inspiring, bold, tenacious, unshakeable, kind, compassionate, non-judgmental, calm, resilient, competent, honest, independent. You name it.

These two categories are self-reinforcing. As you shape your character, you shape your potential in life. As you envision your future, set goals, and take big action steps, you shape your character. You will want to look at both of these things carefully and make some decisions.

But how do you know who and what you should be? Is it just a free-for-all? Randomly choose whatever you think of first?

No, of course not.

Unearth your authenticity. Set out on an expedition to discover *who you really are* and what you want for yourself.

Think about your future and then consider what sort of person you would need to be in order to make the best use of your particular talents, assets, gifts, and strengths. What character traits can be further developed and strengthened to support this vision of who you are becoming? Who do you need to be to accomplish the goals you have set for yourself?

If you find that you are lacking in courage, but you know you will need a lot of it to fulfill your dreams, *put it on the list.* If you have always dreamed of running a marathon, but you can't seem to stick to a training schedule for very long, then you will want to become a person who is *disciplined* and *committed.* If you have a tendency to rely on your romantic partners for more validation than they can give you, it will benefit you to work on becoming *independent, self-reliant,* and more *confident.*

Of course, just deciding on these things will not make them happen. But awareness alone is half the struggle. Identify what you need and want in your life—in your personality and your character—so that you can actively work on developing those aspects.

No, you are not born with your character. You shape it for yourself with your thoughts, your choices, your beliefs, and your actions. So work on doing just that, and you can start with a thought. If you hold a thought or an image in your mind long enough, and if you rehearse it diligently, you will be creating the fertile ground you need in order for those thoughts and beliefs to take shape in your reality.

I have already addressed how we tend to do this all the time, in the negative. ("I'm not good at math," "bad things always happen to me," "the world is full of evil people." Seriously, think about all the things you say in your head about yourself, or about the world. Most of them are probably negative. You need to switch that). The more you lay down paths in your mind that are paved with possibility, the more likely you will get to walk those paths in reality. You will come to believe that they exist.

And, remember, you have to believe it to see it.

If you haven't already done this, you need to start writing some things down. A notebook with pen or pencil is my recommendation, but some people prefer the paperless route and use a phone or computer. Either way, there is no chance of successfully bringing your dreams to fruition if you are not articulating your plan in some way.

Give yourself permission, for a moment, to imagine the perfect scenario of your life. You will have to shift some of these ideas around, depending on how old you are, what you have already done in life, and what's most important to you. If you could live your days any way you want to, what would that look like? (Initially, you can literally have free rein with this. If you want to wake up every morning in a cabin out in the wilderness and spend your days hiking and fishing, then so be it. If you want to be a highly paid trader on Wall Street, with your days buzzing with tension and action, then so be it).

What a lot of people realize when they go to write something down is that they don't really *know* what they would want their life to look like. Often, it's because they don't really know *themselves*. After all, if you have never thought of yourself as the active creator of the events of your life, you wouldn't have known you have choice in the matter, and you wouldn't be accustomed to choosing. If this is the case for you, don't worry. It's actually wonderful to realize this because you now have something to work toward. The mystery of who you are and what you get to choose is not cleared up yet, but you know where to start your investigation.

And what investigation could possibly be more fun? The task of thinking about what you love, what you love to do, where you love to go, who you love to be, and who you love to be with. Sometimes what we think we don't know is more a case of having never clarified it.

Don't be surprised, however, if as you start to think about what you want, you also start thinking about ways to limit yourself. For example, you may be good at saving money, but your spouse isn't and so you start scratching "savings" goals off your list. Or the fact that you have people relying on you (children, elderly parents, sick siblings) causing you to consciously or subconsciously shrink the size of your ambitions because you assume that grandiose plans will never be possible.

You might suddenly feel self-conscious picturing yourself in a palatial mansion rather than a "sensible" apartment. Or driving a Porsche rather than a Honda Civic. And, look, if you have no desire to drive a Porsche, then that's perfectly fine. But if that's your dream car (or whatever your dream car might happen to be), then you need to choose that for yourself.

Regardless of where you are in this process, think some things up and write something down. You can absolutely fine-tune this later. In fact, think of this as a preliminary brainstorming session. I want you to take ten or fifteen minutes (set a timer; the urgency of the time constraint will keep you from editing what you are saying; you want to let everything spill out) and free-write everything that you can think of that you want in this life.

If you feel stuck, you can go back and look at the two pieces of the vision puzzle I wrote about a couple of pages back and just respond to what I suggested in #1: dream job, salary, hobbies, relationships, travel, practices, pastimes, family, education, and so on.

The key here is to find the things that really resonate for you. What would have to happen in your life for you to look back a year from now and say, "Wow, that was a really amazing year!"

It can be because of productive things you did, or things that pushed your boundaries and helped you grow, or just things you've always wanted to do but never made a point to get done.

Now, expand that idea out a bit. What does this show you about what you want from your life, in general? Not just a year from now, but your ideal way of being. Write all these things down.

Go ahead. Do it now. (The next sentences will still be here when you get back).

Ok, welcome back. Take a look at what you've written and consider whether there's a trend, or a pattern, or a theme. Is there something that points you toward a sense of purpose, perhaps? Are you surprised by what you wrote? Have you known these things all along but lacked the chutzpah (or the permission!) to say them? You're going to want to hang onto that piece of paper or save that Word document. This is your start toward a new life, and a more authentic, brilliant, happy, hopeful you.

If you found that you struggled with this exercise, here is what I'm going to suggest: start a journal. Start writing in it every day. Four or five minutes every morning or evening. You can only know what you want if you know what motivates you, moves you, and inspires you. And one of the best ways of figuring this out is to spend some time every day listening to your thoughts and writing them down. William Wordsworth said, "Fill your paper with the breathings of your heart."

If you need some inspiration, I highly recommend the little book by Hal Elrod called "The Miracle Morning." In it, he details a morning routine driven by what he calls the Life S.A.V.E.R.S.—that last word being an acronym for the six practices you can incorporate into your mornings in order to transform your life: Silence, Affirmations, Visualization, Exercise, Reading, and Scribing (a fancy word for "writing," to suit the acronym).

Let's face it, in today's world, with so many gadgets, and distractions, and ways to be instantly gratified, people have lost the art of silence, reflection, and stillness—all of which are means by which we may gain self-knowledge. Without self-knowledge we feel dissatisfied, ill-at-ease, uncertain about our desires and our future, and incapable of making significant changes.

After all, what would we base those changes on? Again, let me reiterate: *if you do not know who you are, you cannot know what you want, or the means by which to attain satisfaction and happiness.* To "know who you are" is not as simple as knowing that you are a teacher, or a parent, or a lawyer, or an entrepreneur. That's not what I'm talking about. I'm talking about developing a deep understanding of what motivates you, fulfills you, feeds you, and invigorates you. You will not necessarily know these things automatically. That knowledge must be sought after and cultivated.

We all want to be fulfilled in our lives. But how does this happen? It isn't accidental, and it isn't arbitrary, and it's different for each person.

One of the "big picture" questions I receive most often from my physical geography students is some variation on "what's the most important thing a person can do to make a difference in the world?" They usually mean it in the sense of environmental issues: resource depletion, global warming, pollution, species extinction, etc.—because these are some of the things we study in that class—but the answer would be the same, regardless of how they mean it. And the answer is this: the biggest impact you can have on the world—in any way, and in all ways—is to strive to become the best, most authentic version of yourself that you can possibly be.

The reason for this is very straightforward and simplistic: when a person diligently identifies, hones, and shares their finest gifts with the rest of the world, everyone benefits. A person who is focused on improving themselves, being of service, creating a life they love, and shining in all the ways they are meant to shine is a happier, more giving, more tolerant, more compassionate, more concerned, more active, and more useful human being. There is no way you *and* the rest of the world won't benefit.

So, what I would say is find what makes you happy. Identify your strengths and take them to world-class level. Be the person you wish you could be if you could be any kind of person at all. Be that good, be that joyful, be that amazing, be that brilliant. The more people who do this, the less people there will be who are angry, frustrated, thwarted, violent, exploitative, demanding, abusive, disconnected, apathetic, and unconcerned. We change the world by changing ourselves. We change the world by coming to know what we have to offer, and then offering it.

Lao Tzu said it best. "If you want to awaken all of humanity, then awaken all of yourself. If you want to eliminate the suffering of the world, eliminate all that is dark and negative in yourself. Truly, the greatest gift you have to give is that of your own self-transformation."

As you are going through the process of learning who you are and letting yourself admit and embrace the things you love, you will assuredly begin to develop some ideas about what you want your "perfect" life to look like. Probably, there are a few things you know for sure, or that you have desired for a long period of time. I want to encourage you to take this a step further, in order to cement the idea that you *do* get to choose, and that the choices are as limitless as your imagination.

I want you to create a vision board.

This can be as simple or as complex as you want it to be, and you can do it in any way that resonates for you. Long before the idea of "vision boards" had taken hold in popular society, my mother taught me a little something about this. For her, a vision board was simply the act of finding pictures that represented something she wanted in her life and taping them to the refrigerator. That's it.

And for her, there was one vision that trumped all the rest: she wanted to live in a house in the mountains.

Let me tell you, at the time she had this vision we were living in a dusty, impoverished desert town riddled with drunks, druggies, and transients. She was the wife of a pastor whose yearly income put him well below the official poverty level. We lived in ramshackle quarters situated behind the church, and we relied on government aid and the good will of the church's parishioners to have food on the table every day. Clothes, and books, and cooking and eating utensils were bought secondhand—if they were bought at all. We had one car, one tenuous income, no rent (we couldn't afford it), meals cobbled together out of whatever was available, and very few prospects of improvement.

And for some unbelievable reason, my mother envisioned herself living in a house in the mountains.

To that end, she cut pictures out of magazines and put them on the refrigerator. And, once a year, she made a point to reserve a spot for the whole family to participate in the "Mountain Homes Tour" of some of the more affluent residents of the mountain community about an hour from where we lived. In a way, I thought she was a bit nuts. But I also understood that she was inspired by looking at these houses, and that it was a deep, heartfelt desire for her to have a residence in the mountains. And the more able we are to picture ourselves in the scenario we most desire, the more likely it is that the scenario will become our reality.

For her, it was a matter of faith—Christian faith, specifically. But I understand now that one can have faith that is not religious and glean the same results. She thought that if she prayed, and believed, and held fast, and created a vision of the life she wanted, and maintained a positive attitude, and spoke affirming words, she would get what she wanted. Regardless of whatever her present circumstances suggested.

And, you know what? She was right. Today, she is living in a house in the mountains, and has been for over 30 years.

When I wanted to have a baby more than anything else in the world, but was plagued by repeated miscarriages, I reluctantly did what my mom had always taught me: I found a picture of a gorgeous baby, and I put it on the refrigerator. The funny thing was, the picture I had chosen was not of one infant, but two: two round-headed beautiful boys. I kept it because it was my favorite picture of any that I had seen; it just had the right "feel" about it.

I didn't end up having twins—as you might be thinking—but I did get my baby: a round-headed boy. Fourteen months later, I gave birth to another one.

Not that the vision, all on its own, created the outcome and ended my struggle with miscarriage. But it *is* what kept me focused and inspired to do what I had to do—no matter what.

At the recommendation of my sister-in-law, I started seeing an acupuncturist. This person suggested that one of the things I could do to begin to prepare my body to sustain a pregnancy was to give up sugar.

Wait…what?

Give up sugar?

I was a serious sugar junkie. As a matter of fact, at that time, my go-to breakfast was a sugary scone or muffin from Starbucks and a cup of coffee—to which I added sugar. Sugary treats were one of my great pleasures in life. Always had been. This crazy acupuncturist was asking a lot.

But I was motivated. *A lot.*

So, I did what she said. I gave up the sugar. All of it. Immediately.

I started eating eggs for breakfast, with toast made from spelt (no added sugar). I took my lunch to work. Sliced meats, string cheese, celery and carrots. On a good day, I could enjoy a banana. I recall lamenting that I ate only to sustain myself; food had lost all its former attraction and joy.

But I persevered. I kept doing it. I looked at that picture on my refrigerator and I knew what I was working toward. It got easier after a while. I learned to like food without sugar. I learned that my chronic sweet tooth was an *addiction* and that, like any addiction, my mind and taste buds were going to rebel until I had established new habits, new preferences, and a new way of being.

After a few months of getting acupuncture, taking some supplements, and eliminating sugar, I became pregnant. And this time I was able to carry to term.

These days, I no longer use the refrigerator as my vision board, but I still use that same method, with the same intention behind it. On the wall behind my computer in the office I share with my husband is a sampling of the things I'm envisioning: a beautiful house with lots of outdoor space for gatherings; a picture of the book table at Costco where I intend my books to take up space someday; the racehorse I wanted to buy shares in (I have since done that); the amount of money I want to make in the year (this is typed out underneath a picture of a stack of money); a nice riding horse; a picture of my husband and I (because I am envisioning the continuation of a wonderful, strong marriage). I used to have a picture up there of my dream car, but I have since purchased it, so I got to take that picture down and replace it with something else.

One of the benefits of doing a vision board is that it forces you to focus. It's not that simply having the vision board causes these things to come to you; it's that if you don't even know what you want, you won't take action in a specific direction, and you won't know where to focus your creative energy. If you're going to put up pictures of things that represent what you want in life, then you have to nail down what that is.

And, by the way, it doesn't have to be physical things. On my vision board, I also have a set of affirmations, as well as "My Top 5 Values" (which, for me, at this point in my life are: authenticity, beauty/wonder, commitment/perseverance/discipline, courage, and gratitude). My vision board is a conglomeration of images and words that represent what I want and who I want to be.

Be as specific as possible with your images, and don't worry that you're blocking the receipt of something better if you haven't nailed down your preferences appropriately. Create the image, the vision, the plan of what you want (or think you want), and then relax. I mean, relax mentally and spiritually. Release attachment. Believe that the best version of what you've "suggested" on your vision board will come to you. But understand: if you have *no* vision (or just the default vision I mentioned before), then your energy is scattered and weak. Your intention will suffer, and your willpower will suffer. You must have a target.

You can't avoid doing the work of learning who you are. The sooner you start, the sooner you can develop and sculpt your authentic self, and the sooner you can achieve your potential and own your brilliance.

To that end, you've got to start sitting in the company of your own psyche, without distractions, and walking through who you are and what you want. What do you think about? What do you care about? What moves you, frightens you, stimulates you, discourages you? Who do you admire, and why? Who would you look to as a model of the attributes you'd like to emulate? Oprah Winfrey, with her courage, tenacity, and penchant for thinking big? Michael Jordan, with his famously disciplined work ethic? J.K. Rowling, who never gave up on her story of a boy wizard named Harry Potter even though it was rejected by 12 different publishers? Maya Angelou whose tumultuous, voiceless past gave rise to a strength of voice nearly unparalleled in modern history?

Think about these things that are meaningful to you, write about these things, and see where it leads you.

Next up: the goals; the struggle; the discipline.

CHAPTER EIGHT

CLIMBING THE MOUNTAIN

*"Discipline is the difference between what you want now
and what you want most."*

~Anonymous

Imagine it: a life you have meticulously crafted for yourself. A life that contains all the components you find most valuable. A life tailor-made for you because it was made *by* you, with an understanding of who you are, what you have to offer, and what you find meaningful. A life that uses your talents, challenges you to grow, and rewards you with good relationships, joyful pastimes, fulfilling work, financial freedom, and deep security.

This is possible. If you are willing to work for it until you achieve it.

Notice I didn't say, work for it until you are tired. Or work for it until you think you've worked enough. I said, work for it *until*.

The somewhat hackneyed saying that "you can achieve anything you want" is mostly true, but there is tenacity and passion implied in that statement. It must matter to you more than food, or rest, or what people think, or designer clothes, or video games, or television shows.

Because, you see, most people aren't willing to give those things up. Most people aren't willing to watch less T.V. or get up earlier in the morning to journal and meditate, or spend their vacation working on their book or growing their business, rather than sunbathing in Hawaii.

And if you think I've just now sucked all the fun out of life with those comments, keep reading.

Think back in your life to the things you find most memorable and/or most meaningful. You probably won't think about the time you binge-watched *Breaking Bad*. You probably won't think about all the days you went to work, came home, and plopped yourself in front of a computer screen and zoned out on videos until it was time to go to bed. It doesn't mean that those things don't have a place; it just means that those are not the activities that are going to move your life forward, and they're not the activities that you find all that amazing, anyway.

The things that are really amazing are the things that either speak to your soul and your authentic interests in some way, or that you had to work really hard to accomplish, or that served someone magnificently, or that get you in touch with gratitude, or that inspire you, or test you, or frighten you, or that you feel are a true reward for your effort.

Meaning is not automatic. It is a natural outgrowth of what you value, but it must be found, acknowledged, or created.

True value and true happiness are derived from hard work that brings us satisfaction, or that has served others well, or that tests and challenges us in some way. Work is good. Having a purpose is good. What that purpose should be is entirely up to you, but without one, we lean toward depression and apathy.

How do you feel when you are focused and working on something that is important to you? Energized. Alive. It's even *fun*.

We are meant to be useful and give value. We are meant to find joy in learning, and creating, and appreciating. That is why we are all born with gifts, and talents, and strengths, and interests. Yes, *all of us*. We feel good when we try hard, and when we bring our best talents and best efforts into the game. We feel good when we know what feeds our soul, and we take the time and effort to pursue it. These things give us pleasure and satisfaction.

They add to our contentment. They soothe and serve us at a very deep level.

So, I would argue that the pursuit of leisure—which we have all given in to at some point, I'm sure—is not so much a way of finding meaning and fulfillment, but a means by which we escape the necessity of those things. Now, don't get me wrong, I'm not against leisure time. Especially as a means of rest and renewal. In this capacity, it is downright crucial. But the pursuit of leisure as a focal point of life—as our main goal—can be hollow and wasteful; a way by which we squander our gifts, rather than making use of them and producing value for ourselves and others.

What this means, then, is that in order to get to a life of profound meaning, deep fulfillment, and immense usefulness, it is necessary to grow in our awareness of ourselves and put in a shit-ton of effort. Effort is difficult. Effort sucks, at times. Effort can be painful. And sustained effort requires the most dreaded word of all: discipline.

But keep in mind: your effort and your discipline, in this case, is primarily for your own benefit—to pursue the thing you love. And to get really good at it. It's to make *your* dreams come true. It's to fulfill your *own* highest potential.

Just think how much effort and discipline you exercise just going to your job every day and putting in an honest day's work. In most cases, it's in service to someone else's business and someone else's dream. Are you just working for a paycheck? I hope not! But if so, wouldn't you rather spend that kind of effort on something meaningful to *you*? Whether you write, teach, play baseball, climb mountains, cook, design clothing, or program computers. When I say that you can craft your own life, I really do mean that the things you love to do can be the focal point of your life and, in many cases, the very way you come to earn your living.

Let's recap for a moment: you're going to start journaling to get to know yourself; you're going to envision the life of your dreams and the person you want to become along the way; you're going to set goals for yourself based on that vision; you're going to act, wherever you are and in whatever situation you occupy currently, as if you are already the person you want to become; you are going to take action every day in pursuit of your goals.

How are you going to maintain all that? How are you going to keep on striving when all that effort becomes painful, unattractive, and seemingly unproductive?

And you must, you know. That's part of the process. That's why so few people meet with wild success and so many don't. You must be willing to do what most people won't do. And that takes discipline. It is easier, after all, to make an excuse (and they can feel so real and so compelling), or to surrender your life to some kind of "fate" than to admit to yourself or anyone else that you just weren't willing to do the hard things.

Or maybe it's not that you're worried that they're too hard—but just uncomfortable or massively uncertain. You stick with the known pleasantness over the unknown potential because you worry that taking on the tough job will cost you the cushy job. Sort of like refusing to break up with the boyfriend or girlfriend who doesn't feel like your soul mate but might be as close as you think you'll ever get.

The reality is: not knowing what's in front of you is scary. Staying in a "safe harbor" may not get you everything you want, but it will at least ensure that you don't lose what you already have. Or so you may believe, anyway.

What you may be doing to yourself, though, could be even worse. If you huddle close to the harbor, seemingly safe, you may not realize that your only hope of salvation and happiness is setting out to sea. If you want to access your highest potential, your greatest dreams, and a life you have deliberately crafted, you must put on the cloak of courage and cut that damn anchor.

How many times have I written that "you must" do something, or you "have to" be a certain way? If you think these repeated insistences are unnecessary or exaggerated, understand that your results will be a reflection of the extent to which you take these exhortations to heart.

The stuff you will need to do, and the practices you will need to put in place are not easy. They are simple, yes; but not easy. I hope this doesn't dishearten you. While visualizing yourself on top of the mountain is absolutely crucial to your journey, the visualization alone will not put you on top of the mountain. You've got to do some climbing for that. Only certain people get to be the ones who stand at the top of the mountain: *those who are willing to climb the hell up it.* Hardly anybody gets there a different way.

The thing is, every time you take a step in that direction, you are becoming more and more the sort of person who could eventually climb the mountain. You don't have to do it all at once. Just a step at a time. And the good news is that discipline is like a muscle; it can be built up gradually. The more you activate that muscle, the better you get, and the more readily you can accomplish what you need to. But it never gets *easy*. A person who trains for a marathon, and then manages to complete one, will not say that it was easy. Only that they understood that it was possible. They still got tired. They probably wanted to quit. Something probably hurt. A lot. But they did it anyway. That's discipline.

How do we get to that level? How do we become disciplined enough to follow through on the things that are important to us and that will add lasting value to our lives?

First, you need to truly understand and buy into *why* you are doing it. If the particular discipline you need to practice is getting up earlier in the morning, but you're not doing something with that extra time that is moving you forward, then it's completely pointless. Why would you continue doing it? It would feel like meaningless torture.

But if you are getting up an hour earlier so that you can do 20 minutes of exercise because you want to change your body and your energy, and 20 minutes of reading because you want to be inspired and heighten your self-development and learn all kinds of ways to be successful in any area of your life, and 20 minutes of journaling because you want to explore your thoughts and discover who you really are, then you've gained a value from what you might first view as a sacrifice. There's a point to it, you can see what it does for you, and it becomes worthwhile.

The same with anything else that requires discipline. Going to the gym; eating better and saying no to sodas and sugar; practicing your craft for 30 minutes a day, every day, no matter what, even if it's at the end of a long work day; saving 10% of your income even if it means you can't stop at Starbucks every day, or you can't buy new clothes very often, or you have to pack a lunch every day when you go to work. For some folks, creating a habit of speaking lovingly to their family, or listening better, or giving up destructive, indulgent habits (like employing "the silent treatment" when they have a conflict with their spouse) takes a *lot* of practice and discipline, but there is a payoff in improved relationships.

Think of discipline as an investment in your future. It's the same as when you set aside money. It might feel like a sacrifice in the moment—you can't buy those shoes you wanted; you can't go to the movies this week— but in the long run, you're buying greater security, greater confidence and, sometimes, enhanced opportunities.

That's what I mean about knowing why you're doing what you're doing. What is the payoff you're going for? How important is it to you? This matters because, psychologically, we have to have the buy-in. We have to be deeply invested in our "why."

Think about this for a moment: when a woman is planning her wedding, often one of the goals—along with all the other things that must be planned and put into place—is to look her best for the big day. (This could apply to the groom, as well, not just the bride). If this involves weight loss, she feels very motivated at this time because she is continuously picturing herself looking beautiful and radiant—and several sizes smaller— as she walks down the aisle in the "perfect" dress she has picked out.

That image is very powerful, and it will cause the soon-to-be bride to do whatever it takes to get there. As soon as she thinks about skipping her workout or going back to her old eating habits—wham! She can figuratively pull that picture up in front of her eyes and know exactly why she is going to stay disciplined.

The trouble here is that as soon as the wedding is in the past, so is the thing that motivated her. She will either need to find another motivator (another vision in her mind) or, better yet, start off with the intention that the "new" person who walks down the aisle is representative of a new lifestyle—a lifestyle committed to health and wellness. The short-term vision can create awesome momentum, but there needs to be a long-term vision in place to keep that momentum going.

For me, finally conjuring the discipline to do the writing I always wanted to do was a matter of getting to a point where I asked myself if there was anything I would truly regret about my life if I found out that I had a terminal illness, for example, and had only a short while to live. The one thing that I thought would really, truly bother me was that, at that point, I had not tried very hard to fulfill my dream of becoming a writer.

If there was ever anything that I really thought I was going to be someday, it was a writer. By the time I was 12, I had already written two full-length manuscripts because writing was just something I loved to do. I wanted to do it all the time. But as I got older, other things drew my attention and other obligations co-opted my time. It wasn't until I was well into my thirties that I really started getting back into it again. But it was way harder to find time to write as an adult than it was when I was a kid and had absolutely nothing else to do. And I was weak. And undisciplined. And easily distracted. And I resented the fact that in order to write, I would have to do it in my "spare" time, which was already limited.

I think I had this idea that there would come some point in my life when I could stop all the other things I was required to do and just become a writer. But I was putting the cart before the horse. In order to be a writer, I had to actually write. And the only way I was going to have the time to write was if I prioritized that part of my life no matter what. Regardless of all the other things I had to do, and in spite of thinking that I had very little time to commit to writing. I had to *act* on my dream, rather than waiting for it to just drift into my hands.

Frankly, I had to get to the point of being fed-up with myself.

I wondered if I was just going to go to my grave without even giving this writing thing a fair shot. Good grief, I had barely tried at all! This one thing that seemingly mattered more than anything else, and I was being totally cavalier about it; carelessly lazy, wishy-washy, and cowardly.

Since I didn't want to see myself as any of those things, and since I still really did have that dream of being a writer, I started to get my act together and put some pieces into place.

And it was hard, by the way, and riddled with failure. And I had to learn how to develop and keep momentum. I had to figure out the role of inspiration in keeping me motivated. I had to incorporate all the things that anyone who really wants to succeed at anything needs to incorporate: visualization, planning, goal-setting, habit-building, accountability, discipline, and an indefatigable love affair with perseverance.

I recall having the experience of reading books on writing and feeling really fired-up and motivated to get some work down. To make *this* time the time that I stuck with it. During the time I was reading such a book, I was excited, engaged, planning my next story, and writing every morning. And it felt *good* to be inspired like that.

As soon as I would finish reading the book that had me so engaged, all the habits that I thought I had put into place would flame out or wither away. In about a day. The inspiration would fade, and with it, the motivation. I would be disheartened. I would think to myself, "that feeling never lasts."

It was perplexing. Distressing.

It caused me to believe that I could never stick to anything; that I was fundamentally lazy, or indulgent, or incompetent.

What it took *years* for me to realize is that the inspiration generated by the book I was reading was a *necessary ingredient* to continued motivation. I didn't understand that I needed to re-energize and re-inspire myself *every single day*, and as long as I did so, I had a much better chance of following through with my ambitions. In fact, I had a nearly 100% chance of following through. I mean, if everything was working great so long as I was reading that book that motivated me, why didn't I just keep on reading such books? So simple, and yet, in a way, I was stubbornly refusing to let myself be "helped" by such a tool.

Zig Ziglar made a humorous point of this problem with his witty words: "People often say that motivation doesn't last. Well, neither does bathing. That's why we recommend it daily."

Just that one little thing! Making sure I had daily inspiration in place. Once I figured it out, I kept at it. I've been doing it for years. Inspiring myself with books—some of which I have read multiple times—and blogs, and videos, and articles, and even certain movies and songs. And I don't just mean inspiration for writing. Inspiration for *everything*. What I didn't realize is that all those books were teaching me how to be successful at *living*. And, yes, this is something we have to learn.

If *learning* is a necessary ingredient to living well, then why do so few people make this a daily part of their lives? It may not primarily be a lack of discipline. Jim Rohn always said, "Things that are easy to do are also easy *not* to do." And maybe people aren't willing to try it because they don't fundamentally *believe* it will make that much difference. Sitting down for 15 minutes every morning with some kind of self-development book. Why should that change their life?

Technically, it shouldn't. But when you read informative topics, you learn. And when you learn, you understand how and why you can do things differently to make desired changes in your life. And that will inspire you to want to make those changes. And when you take action on those desired changes, your life *does* change. But you have to start off with learning how to do it. You can't incorporate a practice you don't know exists. You won't try to expand your beliefs about yourself if you have no inkling of how powerful that can be.

Good habits come about as a result of discipline—but once those habits are established, you no longer need discipline to stick with them. They become a part of your life. Even a necessary and *enjoyable* part of your life. Habits like getting up early every morning and reading for 15 minutes. The world's most successful people are all readers. Oprah Winfrey, Elon Musk, Warren Buffett, Steve Jobs. And that is only a very tiny handful of the vast list. They consume written words for inspiration, education, success, self-development, entertainment, and even to satisfy that wonderful, natural trait called "curiosity." Every single moderately or highly successful person I have ever known (and I can't think of a *single* exception) was a reader. Every single person I have looked up to as a leader, or whose life I admired, or who charted their own course in this world was/is a reader. President Harry Truman famously said, "Not all readers are leaders, but all leaders are readers."

When my husband first set his sights on getting a position as a CEO of a credit union, one of the most important things he did on that road to success was to develop a habit of reading every morning. Just 20 minutes or so. Books on leadership, organizational culture, mindset, self-development. Within a year of starting this practice, he became a CEO.

If discipline is a muscle, then the first and best thing you can do to start exercising it is to get up a little bit earlier than normal every single day and read. Even better if you journal a bit, as well. Or just take a few minutes to plan your day and set some goals. But *definitely* read!

Don't believe me? As I like to say: put it to the test. You can complain that you don't have money for books (though, let me tell you, there are *loads* of free blogs and other content on the internet that can be used for this purpose), or that you are already too sleep-deprived to get up any earlier. Or you can just discount it and let it go. But why not give it a try? What do you have to lose?

Fifteen minutes of your day that, if it works, will start the momentum that could change your whole life.

Isn't it funny, though, how you can feel resistance to *even 15 minutes?* Be careful. That voice in your head that wants to trot out a litany of reasons for why you shouldn't do this, and why it won't work anyway—including the notion that it seems too good to be true—is the same voice that has handed out all sorts of questionable advice.

Don't listen to that voice. Seize the gauntlet I'm throwing down here. Try something different. There is so much knowledge, and wisdom, and direction to be gained. Liberation. Freedom. Fresh air. Take it on.

CHAPTER NINE

THE FUTURE IS SOMETHING YOU CREATE

"Vision is not enough, it must be combined with venture. It is not enough to stare up the steps – we must step up the stairs."

~Vaclav Havel

Once you have a general sense of what you want your life to look like, you need to start taking steps in that direction. Immediately.

It is imperative that you shut your brain down when it wants to offer up excuses that keep you from starting; that keep you from making the changes you will need to make. And, believe me, your brain will do this. *You can't listen.* It's like the devil offering you drugs that will fast-track you to hell. Know that your excuses are the enemy, and that the sooner you take action in spite of those excuses, the better off you will be.

And I'm not kidding here. Wait for it; it's coming. Recognize your uncertainty and excuses for what they are: a set of knee-jerk reactions paying sad homage to the last vestige of whatever is holding you back. They are going to feel real, and compelling, and imperative. Oh, honey, *you are going to want to buy into all of it.*

THIS is the point where you can do something different. THIS is the point where you can take dead-aim at what you want, squeeze the trigger, and say, "NOW!" THIS is the point where courage counts. You must be absolute in your conviction. Clarity comes when you no longer grant power to *any* of your rationalizations.

The reality is, we are prone to establishing a sense of impossibility around certain things. This is why it's so important to start off with creating a vision and managing our thoughts. We have to inundate ourselves with mental pictures of who we want to be so that we become accustomed to seeing ourselves that way—and, thus, wholly accepting of the idea that we *could* be that way. Without this groundwork, taking action in the direction of our dreams is rife with pitfalls.

Can't ever picture yourself as a millionaire? Guess what? Your chances of becoming one just plummeted. Can't picture yourself speaking in front of people? Can't picture yourself finding a hot lover? Can't picture yourself schmoozing with Hollywood bigwigs? Can't picture yourself getting fit? Then guess what?

You guessed it. Ain't gonna happen.

But, then again, just picturing it doesn't make it *magically* happen, either. (Quantum mechanics fans might argue this a little and, for them, I'll put a finer point on it: intention backed by strong emotion loaded with texture, focus, and clarity will still trump simple "picturing" all day long).

You have to take the action required to get there, and you have to consistently, deliberately manage your thoughts. But don't freak out; there are strategies for doing this. I am reminded of an old saying Desmond Tutu quoted once during an interview: "There's only one way of eating an elephant," he reminded his audience. "A bite at a time."

You start somewhere, and you go from there.

Where can you start?

At the beginning. At the beginning of each day. You can decide when you are going to wake up, and you can wake up at that time—without argument, without hesitation, without thought.

Why does this matter? Because you are making yourself do something you don't really feel like doing—and that's what this section is all about. Because most of the things we need to do to get our lives going in a different direction—a better direction—are things that aren't going to kill us; they're just things we find uncomfortable, or scary, or that we believe we will fail at, or that will make us look desperate, or greedy, or God-knows-what.

People who have to make a living selling things—even if it's their forte—know the discomfort of what I'm talking about here. Sometimes it takes a great effort just to offer someone a product, or to suggest an add-on—even if they know it's something beneficial—because no one likes to seem pushy, or false, or dishonest. And no one likes rejection.

But equally problematic is the battle you can get in with yourself. You know you need to exercise more, but you *just don't like it.*

Yeah, so what? Most people would rather eat ice cream than broccoli, but there's a time and place for both. And a ratio. More broccoli, less ice cream, in case that isn't already abundantly clear. More exercising (or just moving around more!) less sitting in front of your TV or your computer.

I'm not here to talk about what you don't feel like doing. I bet you don't feel like going to work, but you go. I bet you didn't feel like going to school every day when you were a kid, but you went. We are all capable of doing things we don't feel like doing. It's just that when we perceive that the choice is in our hands, we are more likely to pass on those things. (And, by the way, the choice is always in our hands, even if we're talking about work or school—but some things *seem* more obligatory than others, and the consequences of *not* doing them, more apparent). In a way, it's the very essence of why we so desperately wanted to become adults when we were kids: we could choose what we wanted to do. No one was going to *make* us do anything.

So, when you find yourself up against something you know you *should* do, but you don't really *want* to do, you might find the little child in you becoming obstinate. Your adult self indulges that little child by simply refusing to do it. Because, as an adult in charge of your own life, you get to. But that's not a good way to operate. Do you really want an 8-year-old at the wheel? It's a pretty good guarantee that you're going to wind up in a ditch.

Believe it or not, starting off with simple things—like getting up at a certain time every day, doing some reading, or walking, or meditating, and making your damn bed—will put you on the road to a better place. Why does this happen? Why does something completely unconnected to where you want to go have such a big impact on whether or not you get there?

Because when you prove to yourself that you can follow-through with a commitment, that you can do the things you don't really want to do, *you prove to yourself that you have control over who you are becoming.* And something else happens, too: you take that background noise off the table. You find clarity. You understand what's important and necessary. And what's *possible.*

And, damn, if you've got control over the little things, why can't you gain control over the big things? Well, the reality is, you *can.* But imagine how you psych yourself out when you realize that you aren't even making yourself get up on time in the morning? (Indulging that little kid inside you again, almost certainly). The big things aren't really any different than the little things—but even the little things can drag us down. That's why doing the little things matters so much.

(If you want to read a great book about how to get yourself to do the things you don't really feel like doing—and I'm sure you do, because you've got to fill those 15 minutes of reading every morning—check out Mel Robbins' *The 5 Second Rule.* You can even listen to it as an audiobook when you're out getting some exercise!)

But here's something else: you've got to be intentional about these habits you're going to create, and the goals you're going to pursue. You can't just wait and see if this little pep talk inspires you to become more productive—accidentally. You've got to select some specific things you want to work on, and then you've got to diligently work on them.

My suggestion—as I've already mentioned—is to start by deciding what time you're going to get up in the morning (pick a time that will leave room for you to accomplish some things before you even start the rest of your day), and then build your goal list out from that.

Pick some things that are important to you. We all have them. We want to eat better, we want to exercise more, we want to build that shed in the backyard. We want to paint the house, clean our closet, and mow the lawn every week. There's always something. You can't escape the simplicity of this. It doesn't have to be the "right" thing. There is no such thing. The idea here is to get you in the habit of taking action on things you want.

Because that's all you're doing when you create the life of your dreams: you're accomplishing the little tasks that will eventually add up to a magnificent whole. Without someone *making* you do it.

Decide what you want to do and set a timeline for doing it. Here are some ideas:

If you want to increase your fitness—or just spend more time moving and less time sitting—you have to set a specific goal around that. You can't just say, "I'm going to exercise more." Here's an idea that will work better.

You could say that you are going to go to the gym for one hour 4 days per week. Or that you are going to walk 20 miles per week or do 10 push-ups twice a day. Set the goal and make a note on some sort of calendar or tracking system when you accomplish it. My calendar is filled with all the things I keep track of. Why? Because it keeps me accountable and it builds momentum. Now, here's the thing: you want to set it up so that you carry these goals over week-to-week. This is another reason why I track everything. And this requires different language when you are setting the goal.

I want to go to the gym, on average, 4 days per week, vs. I want to go to the gym 4 days per week.

This is what I call "flex-fit." If you choose the latter, you will have automatically "failed" if you only go to the gym 2 or 3 days in a given week. If you choose the former, you simply realize that if you only go to the gym 3 days on one week, you need to go 5 on another. You track it all year long. Because if you set certain goals in stone and you miss out *one time* on hitting that goal, you might view that as a failure and give up the whole endeavor. This serves no one. But if you allow yourself a chance for redemption—like, hey, I only wrote 500 words yesterday, but I wrote 1500 words today, thus keeping my 1,000 word-a-day goal intact—then you are much more likely to stick with your plans and reap the benefits thereof.

Another thing you can do is get someone to do it with you. They don't have to physically be with you; they just have to be working toward a goal for themselves. And it doesn't even have to be the same goal! Let each other know what you are working on and pick a time each week to check in with each other.

My husband and I meet with his sister every Friday for what we call "Strategic Planning Sessions." This is when we share our struggles and triumphs for the week, fess-up to which goals we've met, and which ones we haven't, and set some more goals. Some goals don't even get mentioned anymore because we know we are committed to doing those every single week. The beauty of this, though, is that no one wants to come to the meeting constantly offering excuses for why they didn't meet their goals. There's a certain expectation that being able to manage one's own shit is part of what encourages others to manage theirs.

As I've said before, I'm also a firm believer in setting yourself up with daily motivation and inspiration. If I'm trying to change my eating habits, I pick a diet mentor and read their books and use their recipes. (Jorge Cruise was a game-changer for me at one point in my life). If I'm trying to increase my productivity, I've got my books by Brendan Burchard and Dean Graziosi at the ready. If I need to raise the bar and be a badass, it's Jen Sincero. Good, honest, real-time tactics? Mel Robbins. I read this stuff every day. Or listen to it. Every morning while I'm eating my breakfast (and after I've done my 15 minutes of reading), I watch Darren Hardy's "Darren Daily" videos. Just 3 to 5 minutes that help set the tone for the day. All these things give me the energy and inspiration I need to challenge myself and keep moving forward.

Find your fuel and let it energize you. This is why the reading that I mentioned in the last chapter is so important. So, line that reading up with whatever it is you want to accomplish: gardening, diet, meal-prep, improved relationships, saving money, making more money, becoming courageous, or authentic, or accepting. There are books on productivity, habit-building, exercising, investing, strategizing, chicken-raising (I had a period of time when I did *that*, too!).

Now, ultimately, this isn't about just these little goals. When you start setting goals, and taking action, and making improvements in one area of your life, it will give you the confidence to do it in other areas. And it's not just confidence that you gain from it. You start to learn more about courage, and discipline, and accountability, and the strategies you can use for pushing yourself to do things you don't feel like doing.

Look, if you want to lose weight and get in better shape, you *cannot* continue to do whatever it is you've been doing that got you in the spot you're in. You have to change something. And that's hard. Hell, if it wasn't, you would already be doing it.

The reason you don't exercise every day is because *there is something else you want to do more*. Even if it's just the work you feel you need to get done. (You may tell yourself that you simply don't have time, but is it true? Is it a TV show that you're choosing over the new lifestyle? Is it the evening out that you tell yourself you "deserve?" Those 30 minutes more of sleep? Sure, some people really *do* have a hard time fitting something else in, but most of us simply have that *belief* rather than the actual circumstances. We all have the same 24 hours in a day. What we do with that time is a matter of *prioritization*).

For example, most of us really do like salads, but we just might like an enchilada, chips, and salsa even more. We might want to end a crappy relationship, but we really want someone to go out to dinner with on Friday nights.

Recognize what you're choosing and why. You may even be very good at rationalizing your situation. You'll tell yourself that you'll start your diet tomorrow rather than today. What difference does it make? Or, compared to the amount of TV you *used* to watch, you're doing way better. I absolutely understand that, in the moment, you often don't want to do what you know you should be doing. But get past the "I don't want to do it," feeling and ask yourself again: *what am I trying to accomplish?* Which of these do you want more: the gratification in the moment, or taking a step toward your goal? This is a decision that only you can make.

And this is how it is. But you break the old patterns in moment-to-moment choices. I can tell you that it will be uncomfortable. You will find resistance cropping up disguised as fine and compelling reasons against making change. There will likely be a million things against you, including friends and family who resent or sabotage your better choices because it makes *them* uncomfortable. Try to think of it as a changing trajectory that takes place one miniscule shift at a time. Each choice nudges the trajectory in the way you want it to go. As you get better at making better choices, they become less monumental and painful, and more habitual. And that means they get easier. In the long run, the victories you accomplish will blow your mind.

So, I want you to get real for a second. When you look at all the aspects of your life, do you feel adequately fulfilled in each of them? Work, relationships, character, recreation, health, fitness, education? (The aspects that constitute "fulfillment" will be unique to you). If not, do you want to be?

I'm going to assume that there are things in your life that are not quite working, and you'd like them to work better. Or, they're working really well, but you've never challenged yourself, and you'd like to see what else you're capable of if you did.

I don't know why it is—and maybe we need a psychologist, or biologist, or philosopher, or theologian to answer it—but I think most of us have a sense of our own intrinsic potential, and whether or not we are acting in accordance with it.

In other words, do you fundamentally feel that you *could* be doing more or doing better than you are? I'm not talking about an inferiority complex. And I'm not talking about the guilt you might feel from society telling you all the things you "should" do. Let that shit go. I'm talking about the sense that you have sold your soul somewhere along the line; that you are not being your authentic self; that you are not shining the way you were meant to shine. It's a personal thing. It's unique to you. That feeling causes a void inside; a sense of loss. Maybe a sense of self-sabotage. And from time to time you wonder: what if I stopped holding myself back? What if I really went for it? How high could I rise? How great could I be? What kind of life could I create for myself?

Well, here's your chance to find out.

Start out with just setting the *intention* of challenging yourself. That is, creating a template of possibility. What, indeed, *could* you be?

I love rituals—actually, human beings in general are predisposed to desiring, appreciating, and benefiting from rituals—and one that you can add into your life right away is the ritual of *planning*. Planning your week, for starters. Setting aside an hour or two on a weekend day (or some other day when you are off work) when you are able to focus on the task, and then getting out your notebook and strategizing about the coming week. You can divide this into two sections: "things to do" and "goals". They are very different.

Your "things to do" list is all the stuff that you have a certain urgency about getting done—often stuff related to your job. It helps to write these things down because it allows your brain to stop trying to hold onto them, thus freeing up mental space for other, higher-level thought processes.

My job as a teacher requires me to do a lot of work outside my normal "working hours"—like grading, and lecture prep, and research, and a variety of other tasks. These I write down as a "things to do" list, and I make a strong effort to limit these activities to certain days of the week, or certain hours of the day, so that they don't consume *all* my time. (They so easily could if I let them!)

So, what I'm talking about are the things that you have to do because your job requires them, or your kids require them (if, for example, you need to make medical and dental appointments, or remember the events you need to drive them to), or regular home and lifestyle upkeep requires them (laundry, cleaning the bathroom, doing a water change on the aquarium, and so on). These can be things you don't even normally write down because they are rather routine for you, but I would write them down for three reasons: #1) you can have the satisfaction of crossing them off during the week as you accomplish these tasks, #2) you don't have to worry about forgetting them and having them sneak up and bite you in the ass later, and #3) you can separate them out from the tasks you need to do that will move you forward in your life and raise your game.

And that's the next list I want to talk about.

This list is your "goals" list. These are the things you want to accomplish that are either *not* related to your job, or are related in a non-obligatory, non-urgent way.

For example, if you are a manager in a company, you may want to—along with all your routine responsibilities—hire a leadership coach to enhance your game and make you a more valuable player, so to speak. These tasks—the hiring of a coach, and all the work that you would do around that—would be listed among your "goals," as opposed to "things to do." You don't *have* to do it. It's not breathing down your neck, and you won't lose your job if you don't do it. But could it potentially launch you to that *way* higher position that you've been dreaming of? Heck yes.

If you own a sales business and you are spending all your time filling orders and keeping up with records and receipts, but you have no time to do additional advertising, innovating, and marketing to grow your business, you are stuck in "things to do" and not making the most of possible "goals."

My "goals" list will have everything related to my writing on it: how many words I'm going to write per day or week, what editing tasks I have to do, which people I have to hire at what time for which job. If I'm doing a writing workshop, my goals associated with that will be included. My health and fitness goals. My recreation goals. My coaching goals. Notice there is nothing associated with teaching on here—*except* in those instances where I have long-term tasks to accomplish that I want to avoid procrastinating on (like performing Student Learning Outcome assessments and modifying curriculum outlines), or if I have additional things I've decided to take on (like conferences, or speaking engagements, or learning about teaching at the prison).

During your weekly planning sessions, you are going to separate out these things and make different lists. Create an enjoyable ritual of it. Sit in your favorite spot, pour yourself a cup of coffee or a glass of wine, use a journal that you keep just for this purpose, and grant yourself the honor of actually *planning* your future.

I like to have a plan for my year, a plan for each week (usually made on Friday, for the following week), and then a plan for each day. The daily plan can be made at the same time you make your weekly plan (by breaking your week down into daily goals), or you can do your daily plan at the start of each day. Either way, there is tremendous power in being intentional about the activities you are going to include in your week, and the ways in which you are going to take control of your time and your life and move yourself forward.

At first, you may struggle to create "big picture" goals, and you will find yourself focusing on things that are close at hand. That's OK. Once you start getting on track with the most obvious of your desires—like losing weight, or starting to save money, or finding a better job—then you will almost certainly come to realize that there is a bigger picture you may have been missing out on. Focusing on what kind of *job* you want turns into wondering what kind of *career* you could have, and what sort of occupation or project or business would make the best use of your talents, and ambitions, and would provide the lifestyle and life-situation you most desire.

Eventually, those things you once struggled to do—eat right, exercise, plan your day, set goals and achieve them—become *habits*, and your brain finds pleasure in being stretched and challenged, and the next thing you know, it's not a question anymore of, "can I get off the couch?" It's "how can I change the world?" And you will really believe that you can. And the goals you set will start to reflect this new expansion of your mind and your confidence.

I believe, with deep conviction, that we change the world—all of us— by bringing our best selves to the table. By bringing our brilliance onto the stage.

We all have it.

Those things that you love, that stuff that you're good at, that way of being that you admire in yourself (even if you do it self-consciously and quietly); that is the *you* that is meant to shine. Over and over, people cover this up. Too shy to bring it forth. Too ashamed of other parts of themselves. Too uncertain or fearful of the reaction.

What does it serve you to sit still and let life happen to you? Can't you put yourself out into it, heart open, arms wide, eager to see what you are capable of? What would you do differently if you believed the future was something you actively *created*, and not just something you lived into mindlessly and powerlessly?

Think about where you want to go, and who you want to be. Visualize that person. Figure out what actions are required to become the person you want to be. Make a roadmap of those actions and give yourself a timeline. Then start setting goals that you can work toward, even just a little bit every day. Share these goals with a friend and ask them to hold you accountable. Read materials that inspire you and drive your ambition and teach you which actions to take. Do it every day. *Make it a habit.* Read these things repeatedly. There are so many things we learn, and then forget and have to be reminded of. Self-development is a journey, not a destination. Commit to doing it for life. Understand why that matters.

CHAPTER TEN

ALL YOU CONTROL IS YOU

"Hatred is never appeased by hatred in this world.
By non-hatred alone is hatred appeased.
This is a law eternal."

~The Buddha

Take a deep breath.

We need to talk about something.

There's a little secret that a lot of people don't know, and which makes a big difference. It's this: you can't create your best life with one hand while plotting the destruction of someone else with your other hand. You can't demonstrate your own virtue by damning your nemesis to hell. You can't rejoice in your enemy's pain and still make the case that you're taking the high road. You also can't hold onto the thought that the actions of other people are the reason you aren't where you want to be in life.

As you become a person who is dedicated to changing your thought patterns, to owning your brilliance, and to developing and honoring your finest character, you become less and less a person who allows their focus to be distracted by the various "evils" of the world—in whatever way they manifest. You also become more capable of recognizing those evils for what they are: the sad tragedy of individuals disconnected from and unaware of their higher selves.

It is a very human propensity to be caught between wanting to think higher thoughts and improve one's sense of self-responsibility and self-love and at the same time, to still feel the need to place blame in a sort of left-handed fashion. Those darker, lower sensibilities seem to have a way of creeping in through the back door.

For example, the woman who explains how a divorce has freed her, and how she has more self-worth and self-respect, and then goes on to rail about what a rat her ex-husband is and how much he damaged her life.

Or the man who says he has learned to enjoy being single because it is teaching him self-confidence and different coping mechanisms, and then follows this up with the statement that you can't trust anyone, anyway, and relationships aren't worth the pain they cause.

Or the person who says, "I have finally learned to love myself. Too bad no one else loves me."

Or, "I want to believe in the goodness of people, but I am constantly being let down."

Do you see how, in each of these examples, the first part is positive and affirming, and the second part knocks the feet out from under the first part?

Leaves a bit of a bad taste in your mouth, doesn't it? There's this sense of dissonance; something isn't adding up.

When we think about a person whose light is shining and whose life is a testament to their inner work and their outer discipline and perspective, we don't think of someone who is negative, manipulative, or has a victim mentality.

You cannot achieve your highest potential while being petty, vengeful, and unforgiving. Your joy, or your success, or your ability to make your own way in the world should not be dependent on what happens (or doesn't happen) to someone else. ("I'm happy because I know they're going to get what's coming to them." None of your business. Not your concern. Focus on *you*. One hundred percent. No exceptions). What you want for yourself, you must want for others. Wishing ill on another person—even if they've wronged you personally in some way—will not advance your overall satisfaction or success in life. It might temporarily satisfy your desire for anger or resentment, but it will not build your character and positively shape your future. In fact, it will do the opposite. It will mire you in bitterness and stifle your forward momentum.

I know. There are times in our lives when we are rocked by heartache. When someone we trusted betrays us, or when things just didn't go the way we would have hoped. When our hurt and loss morphs into anger and vindictiveness. Or it renders us seemingly helpless and hopeless for a while. Take some time when this happens. Let yourself feel it. All the way down to the bitter dregs. Grieve. It's important to allow this. But you can't relinquish your agency—your ability to act independently and exercise free choice—just because you've taken a hit at the hands of someone else. You *still* have the power to determine outcomes. You mustn't become enrolled in a limiting mindset or limiting self-image.

When you suggest that the actions of others are to blame for the reason you are in a situation, it shifts the responsibility off you and onto someone else. Even if they *are* to blame for something, you alone are still responsible for how you move forward, and what you make of it. (We'll talk about perspective in the next chapter).

Because what would it be like if someone else *was* responsible for your life? Either *you* are the one steering the ship, or you aren't. Which do you think it is? If you think someone else is steering *your* ship, you better grab that wheel back. And don't say you hope they smash against the rocks as you're doing it. You see? Go on about your business. The rest doesn't concern you.

I'm not suggesting there aren't ways in which other people impact our lives, and even make them more difficult or dangerous. Usually, if a person is toxic, or we feel that they're "ruining" our life, we have the choice to get away from them. If a person is influencing a situation from outside our control, or if the choices of others are hurtful, then we still have to "manage our shit," as I like to say, from the place where we do have power—which is over our mindset, our choices, and our actions.

We cannot control other people. Therefore, our position of power is only and always within ourselves. You may have even had the experience of someone shutting *you* out of their life, believing *you* are the toxic one. Sometimes they are right (we have to admit that and acknowledge that this may be a healthy choice for them), and sometimes they are not right. Sometimes they are being influenced by other people who have an axe to grind, or some other agenda. Or by their need to perpetuate their belief that they are a victim. Regardless, I will say it again: we do not control other people, only ourselves. All the work that we can possibly do is within ourselves. Others have to do their own work, and we must let them.

Certainly, we can try to understand their perspective. We can make sure we are responding to them (when such a response is necessary) from our highest selves—that is, as the person we would *like* to be, where it is not our lowest nature on display, but our highest. A place of compassion, perhaps, or even just a steady, solid assurance of each person's inherent value and their right to freedom of thought and belief.

Viewing the world through a lens of fear, or powerlessness, or through a lens that assumes the evil nature of humanity is counterproductive and can even be debilitating.

It will make us angry and fuel the fire of our thoughts that circle around injustice, and victimization, and helplessness. And when we focus on these things, we are not choosing our own path, or seeking solutions, or seeing these things as obstacles that can be overcome but as obstacles that will eventually overcome us. And then our minds and our souls become contaminated with the bitter poison of hatred. It feels justified. Because we have been harmed, or mistreated, or because there is grave abuse of power in the world. We want to rail against the pain, or against the people or systems that have caused the pain. Or caused the struggle. Or made the struggle harder. But as the quote at the start of this chapter says, "Hatred is never appeased by hatred in this world. By non-hatred alone is hatred appeased." Martin Luther King, Jr. said something similar: "Yes, it is love that will save our world and our civilization, love even for enemies."

There's no getting around this. There's no getting *out* of this.

Ask yourself this: Is hatred useful? Is it creative? Does it build, or heal, or justify? Does it expand our consciousness, or awareness, or capacity to change and grow? No. None of these things. It is driven by powerlessness and fear. It is born out of feeling wronged, or mistreated, or taken advantage of, or misunderstood. But it does not fix these things. It doesn't change them. It is fundamentally damaging and destructive. And victim #1 is yourself.

But what if you could eliminate the object of your hatred? Or hate them into subjugation? Drive them, in your hate-filled zeal, to see the error of their ways? You could look to Rwanda as a model. The Hutu tried to hate the Tutsi right out of existence, and they nearly succeeded. Nearly 1 million men, women, and children murdered—most of them hacked to death with machetes. That's a lot of hatred.

Did this solve the problem for the Hutu? Did this make them better people? Did this prove to the world that the Hutu were right, and the Tutsi were wrong? Did this make Rwanda a better nation?

No. Of course not.

Did this solve the problem for Germany? Was the murder of 6 million Jews really "the final solution?" Heavens, no.

You might not want me to try to talk you out of your hatred. If your child, or parent, or friend was killed by a drunk driver, for example, you might believe you have every right to hate the person who is responsible. And, yes, you do have that right. But does it change anything? Does it solve anything? Does it serve you in the long-term?

To be honest, and given the example I just offered, even if we know on an intellectual level that our hatred will not be of service to ourselves or anyone else, I doubt if anyone among us could say that they would know just how to overcome it and redefine their life going forward.

However, I can write here unequivocally, that if there is any part of you that is longing to heal and create renewed purpose for your future, you will need to move through your hatred and/or your despair. Feel it—because you're going to feel it—and then do everything in your power to move past that place of misery and stagnation. Recovery is a process that takes time. And, often, the help of others. Allow it, and then begin the exploration and acceptance of whatever is still waiting for you on the other side of that recovery. Or even *because* of that recovery. You have to. Hate can do nothing but destroy. It will either destroy the object of your hatred, or it will destroy you. And if the former, then the latter is not far behind.

No one can say they wouldn't feel horror and hatred if they found themselves in some hideous situation that was perpetrated by evil. But, in the end, would you want that feeling to rule you? To govern your life? To determine everything that you will ever be? Probably not. You have to decide what you want, and what you stand for. To feel better, eventually? Lighter? To experience renewed purpose in your life? If so, then moving off the path of hatred, revenge, bitterness, and resentment is absolutely necessary. You have assuredly seen people overcome grief and do better. It's just that at this moment, you may not know how to get to that point.

And in the end, what is the payoff, after all, for feeling hatred? Is it to feel as if we are "punishing" someone? Your punishment is lost on them. Is it to protect your heart? You may succeed in that, but a closed heart has not only lost the capacity for pain—but also for joy, and love, and connection.

We must find the place where our wounds are the pathway to understanding and healing—not the place from which we strike out because we are vulnerable. If we can do that, we can break that cycle where we subconsciously feel justified in doling out retribution because we, ourselves, have been hurt.

But that's the trick, isn't it? How do we do that?

Remember what I talked about? About choosing the characteristics you want to see in yourself? You are basing those characteristics on the person you see as your highest self. How would that person respond to injustice? To pain?

If you don't know, then that's some of the work that needs to be done. You see, this is how people can change the world by changing themselves. When you are consciously making a bold stab at creating your own life, and choosing who you are going to be, every moment of every day, you are not going to be so easily triggered emotionally by the things that anger you, pain you, or irritate you. You cannot choose what happens, but you can *always* choose how you react. If you are not choosing—if your responses are automatic—then you are not bringing enough awareness to them.

As you bring your mind into a place where you can direct the trajectory of your thoughts, and when you calm the roiling undercurrent of your emotions, you can allow compassion to take the place of fear. You can allow forgiveness to take the place of hatred. You can imagine yourself as a solid rock with the waves surging around you. It isn't that you don't feel anything, it's that you do not allow yourself to get *triggered* by the storm around you. You are centered, and safe, and solid in yourself. You are confident because you have done the work that fosters it. You know you can act with courage because you have practiced doing so in small ways, over a long period of time.

Each of us is responsible for the energy we put out into the world, and the tone we bring to our interactions. Will it be cynicism, sarcasm, condescension, judgment, indifference, impossibility, arrogance, intolerance, blame, and frustration?

Or will it be kindness, clarity, compassion, equanimity, responsibility, accountability, cooperation, honesty, encouragement, acknowledgment, and respect?

You get to choose who you are going to be and how you are going to behave. When you approach situations from this perspective, you don't have to wonder, "What will I do when 'this' comes up", or "What will I do when 'that' comes up?" The question is only: who will you *be* moment by moment, every day of your life?

When you know the answer to *that* question, then you know the answer to all the others.

PART TWO:

PERSPECTIVE

CHAPTER ELEVEN

MIND OVER MATTER

"It's not what you look at that matters; it's what you see."

~Henry David Thoreau

In a way, it is easy to write about the necessity of focusing on possibility rather than impossibility. It is easy to point out how limiting beliefs can limit our reach in life, and how we must train our brains to generate positive thoughts and words. These are conceptual ideas; they make sense on paper. But what does this practice really look like, where do we encounter the pitfalls, and how do we learn to accept and appreciate the struggle?

This is where it becomes important to learn about *perspective*. You know the adage: "hindsight is 20/20." We have all said it. We all understand *why* it gets said. Because we have all experienced situations where if you knew in the moment of an event or a decision *what you would come to know somewhere down the line*, you would either have made a different decision, or you would have experienced a certain peace or acceptance toward what was happening.

For example, a woman whose husband divorces her and then she finally meets the love of her life two years later. At the time of the divorce, all she can feel is pain. All she can experience of the situation is that it's awful. But later she comes to realize that it wasn't a bad thing at all; it was just that her *perspective* was limited at the time she was experiencing the event.

Of course, you can't fast-forward to the future and take a peek at how things in your life are going to turn out. The interesting thing, though, is that most people behave, in the midst of a trying situation, as if the only possible outcome is a bad one.

And even when we know that a *good* outcome is likely, how often do we use that knowledge as leverage to help us respond gracefully and positively to our struggles? Maybe not as often as we could, to say the least.

The reality is, we can always choose what perspective we want to take, even if we don't know any outcomes. And this is because we can always choose our thoughts, and what we are going to focus on. What this means, effectively, is that what goes on in our inner world will constantly be having an impact on how we perceive our outer world, and how we perceive our outer world determines, in large portion, our reality—regardless of specific circumstances, situations, or conditions.

Picture for a moment a scene in which you are driving down the highway on the first day of your vacation. You probably feel light-hearted— even euphoric—as you notice the contrast of the white clouds in the blue sky, the shadows that accentuate the crevices in the mountains, the nuance of color between brush and trees and grass. Everything looks beautiful, your body feels relaxed, and you even have more patience toward the other drivers on the road.

But put those same circumstances on a "normal" day when you are driving to work, and you will likely see it all differently. Instead of noticing the beauty around you in fine detail, you are probably entirely oblivious to it. Instead, you have a knot forming just beneath your sternum, and you are thinking about all the trials of the day ahead of you, and how you will make it through. Indeed, you may even be thinking of how best to break your day down into its most manageable components so that you can effectively get to the end of it.

That's not a bad strategy, of course, if your intention is to just get this day under your belt, like any other item on your checklist. But what you have lost is the experience of *the day, itself.* You are not happy, you are not excited, and you are not enjoying the many moments that could make the day worthwhile to you. Your potential enjoyment of the day is tempered by the stress of your job, or even your distaste for doing it. Instead of focusing on things that you could enjoy, or even infusing a sense of purpose into your work (which is possible in almost *any* job), your entire goal is simply to reach the end of the day and go home.

Imagine this, though. What if, just as you arrive to work, you get a text from a family member. It says the following: "Guess what? Uncle Greg left all of us $20,000 each in his estate! It's being dispersed this Friday. OMG, can you believe it?" Suddenly, you shift from despair and anxiety into quasi-ecstasy, even though the content of what you will encounter in your day at work will not have meaningfully changed because of this news. But the way you *feel* has changed. Your psychology has changed. Your perception of your reality has changed. Because now you feel like you have something to look forward to, and so the trials you are faced with on this day will suddenly not look so daunting. You will get through them. They are just incidentals.

In these above examples, the way you experience your day is dependent on your perspective. In the first example, the fact of being on vacation has caused a feeling of benevolence that would not be present if you were driving down the same highway to go to work. On the other hand, the second example shows that even the experience of work can be shifted because of some other change in circumstances that causes you to feel differently about your day.

What I'm suggesting is that we choose our perspective regardless of our circumstances. *Choose* to enjoy your beautiful surroundings *even if you're going to work*. *Choose* to do your work with a positive attitude even if you don't have $20,000 waiting for you on Friday.

And I will say this, also. When you are creating the life you want, your perspective will automatically start shifting on a day-to-day basis. Having something meaningful that you are aiming for (a bit like having Uncle Greg's $20,000 at the end of the week) will change the way the journey feels to you. You will begin to appreciate the steps of the journey because you are creating it yourself as you go along, and because you know it's not a dead-end.

An experience I had in Iceland several years ago may be helpful in illustrating how we can choose our perspective in various situations, and also reinforce our understanding of the ideas about possibility, authenticity, and self-knowledge addressed earlier.

My trip to Iceland was for the purpose of hiking the famous Laugavegur Trek with a group of friends. We had previously become well-acquainted on a "walk across Wales" wherein we covered 137 miles in the span of 10 days, thus triggering my husband to jokingly refer to all my subsequent trips with this group of people as "death marches."

When we were choosing our next destination, the reason I voted for Iceland had nothing to do with anything I knew about this northern country at the time. It was literally a spontaneous gut reaction to what I perceived as a most spectacular challenge. So, I can tell you from the start that the very fact of *being* in Iceland in the first place was a result of taking action on a feeling that I couldn't help but believe represented the best within me: a courageous, impulsive draw toward the thing that deeply *resonates* in spite of all normal reason that says it really shouldn't. (And these things, by the way, that elicit your curiosity and your passion are things that should be paid attention to; they will point you in the direction of your happiness and fulfillment).

Iceland, as far as I knew, was a land of cold and desolation, and yet I wanted to go there more than I've wanted almost anything. Would it be appropriate to say that it *called* to me? That is what it felt like. (Again, these things are important. *Tune in to your inner self and listen to those callings*).

And yet, the first day of this deeply desired trek had mostly been a long day of waiting.

We waited at bus stops for our transportation to arrive, and then we waited on those buses over miles and miles of roads that took hours to traverse. We waited at the trailhead for our guide and the two missing

French Canadians (who had decided to go on a hike before the hike, as unlikely as that might sound). We waited for bathrooms, for lunch, for instructions on what to eat at the table and what to take in our packs with us. Then, we waited for maps, and photos, and the counts, and re-counts, and the shuffling of some trekkers from one group to another. But, finally, there was the moment when the waiting was over, and we started walking; when we shouldered our packs for real and set out in a somewhat-single-file configuration for a line of hills that rose from the green valley floor.

At any given moment, it was hard to decide what my dominant emotion was: trepidation, anxiety, excitement? There were legitimate reasons to feel all these things. So many people I didn't yet know, nostalgia for my husband and kids, worry over my mother—who was about to undergo surgery back home—the vast uncertainties along the trail. Was I fit enough? Did I bring the right gear? What did the guide mean by "river crossings"? Would my camera battery die? Would there be enough to eat?

But there was also love of adventure, excitement for the journey, an open heart toward my new friends, exhilaration over the wide-open and desolate landscape; curiosity, and wonder, and hopefulness.

A sensation crept over me; a familiar one. Within it, wrapped up like a gift, was a single word: *choose*.

What feeling did I *want* to have? What experience beckoned me the most deeply? What values of mine had so trumped all others that I found myself climbing a mountain in the southern part of Iceland through snow, and ice, and moss so thick it could hold a prone body like a mattress? I realized, with absolute conviction, that *that* was the feeling I needed to focus on.

It was a tight bundle of love for adventure, and challenge, and beautiful landscapes, and physical exertion, and camaraderie. It was the best feeling in the world to me, and I had traveled to a far corner of the earth in pursuit of it.

Why would I sell that sensation for the petty musings of things that could go wrong? In the very midst of the thing I most wanted, I was letting my focus and energy drift to things I *didn't* want. And I realized that it had occurred because it was a habitual action.

Yes, a *habit.*

A habit to worry. A habit to be anxious. A habit to think negative thoughts. A habit to run through the litany of possible poor outcomes, and what I would do if they should come up. And all that thinking about these things was stealing my focus from the moment at hand and forming a knot in the center of my chest.

Can you relate? Has this ever happened to you?

What a waste.

But what if I could shift my thinking? *What if we can always shift our thinking?*

And it turns out, I could. As we climbed steadily from green meadows and gurgling streams into a more barren and cold landscape, I shut out any voices that would rob me of a single, glorious sensation on this first day. I had the amusing thought that the mountain range we were climbing, with its light brown coloration draped in white snow looked very much like a Bundt cake drizzled with vanilla frosting. That's the last thing I remember noticing before the surprising steepness of the climb and the level of exertion claimed my full attention.

When the trail leveled out and we all allowed for a brief pause, I took in my surroundings with awe. Brown hills streaked with pastel pink and blue, black volcanic outcroppings, snowbanks on thick layers of gray-green moss, and steam floating from fumaroles under melting glaciers. The air was crisp, and a breeze fanned us gently.

With the burden of anxiety lifted by my own desire to shift my thinking, I felt an astonishing—indeed, breathtaking—sensation that my chest was expanding remarkably and that my conscious awareness had broken out of a bond. I relaxed my arms at my sides and tilted my head back so that my vision could include the cloud-flecked sky. I thought: "I have never been so happy in my life."

Wow! From feeling tight and anxious to expansive and ecstatic—all because I changed my perspective on what I was experiencing by changing the thoughts I was allowing myself to think. As Kahlil Gibran put it, "The appearance of things changes according to the emotions; and thus we see magic and beauty in them, while the magic and beauty are really in ourselves."

But there was something else wrapped up in that sensation: not only did I feel amazingly happy, but I realized that it was a pivotal moment in understanding what happiness felt like for me, and a chance to consider how I could achieve that more frequently. Indeed, how I might achieve happiness, in general.

And this is what I mean about *possibility*: there are moments in life when we brush up against *what might be*, and sometimes it is so fleeting that it is painful—because it is like something we almost had but which slipped through our grasp. And, often, we don't even know the nature of it; only that it creates longing.

Certainly, if my own tendency was to relinquish my happiness to the thieves of negativity and anxiety, then it was not surprising that when I chanced upon the possibility of elevated thought and a profoundly satisfactory existence, I would worry about the fleeting nature of it.

It was important for me to have that realization that a great deal of what I experienced in my life was a reflection of the thoughts I was thinking, and where I was putting my focus. Not that I would fail to think *good* thoughts when circumstances looked bad (which is important, of course) but that I would actually choose to think *bad* thoughts when circumstances were even what I would consider ideal.

There is more to this story, though, and this was not the end of my lessons in Iceland.

As we hiked onward in that first day of our trek, the brown, hill-like mountains gave way to more rugged terrain, higher in elevation. In Iceland, in the summer (especially after a particularly cold winter), what this means is snow. Lots of it. Not falling on us but covering the trail and requiring us to make our way through it. Our guide told us this was unusual. That, in fact, the hut we were hiking to had only been accessible for about two weeks (and it was already August!). Here, I would encounter all the demons of my previous thoughts.

The snow stretched in front of me, seemingly interminably. I could not tell where the snowy landscape ended and the cloudy sky began. My boots felt wrong, and my feet were getting wet; my knees started hurting, setting in motion those wheels of worry again; I was hungry and tired and had no idea how many miles we would have to trek before any of those issues would be resolved.

And yet…I had not forgotten the previous lesson of the day. It became a challenge to continually re-focus my thoughts on something other than the desire to complain. After all, the challenge—on the big scale of things— was quite small. There *would* be food and rest, eventually. We *would* reach the first hut, and no one's life was or would be in danger. *And I was in Iceland!* The foolishness of being anything other than euphoric over my circumstances was not lost on me.

So, I did what I could do to manage the situation: I went to a place inside my mind and I created, for my physical self, a simple task to occupy each moment. I looked down at the snowy trail (scarcely a trail, I should point out, as we were creating it as we went along) and concentrated on placing each foot as closely in the path of the previous hiker as I could. This reduced the strain on my knees, since every misplaced footfall in the deep snow wrenched against my joints and muscles. And it gave me something to focus on. Then I counted: one, two, three…all the way to one hundred. When I reached one hundred, I looked up.

The distance was undiminished, but maybe a cloud had moved. Back down went my head: one, two, three…another hundred, another glance upward. I felt that we were walking *into* the sky. Our elevation was such that there were no peaks above us, and I could not see anything past my view of the horizon. It was almost eerie.

I kept at my task for I don't know how many counts of one hundred—for far more than I had anticipated. But I remember feeling grateful that I wasn't cold; that the exertion kept me cozy warm, that I had chosen to wear my boots rather than my trail runners that day, and that I wasn't walking through the snow alone. I slipped into a trance-like walk; counting, looking up, counting. In an unexpected moment, someone shouted that the huts were just over the next rise, and I had the thought: *already?*

When coats and boots were shed, and sleeping bags were doled out, and bunks claimed, we had the sheer joy of sitting down to a heavenly meal (because all meals are heavenly when one is hungry and far from home), and a glass of wine, and the raucous laughter of new and old friends, and I had yet another realization: part of what made the evening so deeply satisfying was because of the challenge it took to get there.

Not just the hike through the snow. Not just the long bus rides, and the waiting, and the shortage of food, and the uncertainty that almost always comes from embarking on any adventure. It was also the courage it took to dream a dream of trekking in Iceland, to believe I could come up with the money, and the time away, and the blessing of my family. To board a plane and fly across an ocean and don a pack and hike through snow and not stop because there may be glacial rivers to cross on foot and precipices to crawl past and volcanoes to ascend that sometimes required one to hang onto ropes or chains (and all of that did, in fact, come to pass).

That first evening in the first hut was magnificent because it contained within it all those things. Because it was the culmination of thinking that something outlandish and even impossible, by some standards, had entered into my consciousness as something *possible*, and I had proven it to be so. To get there was exciting—but also hard, and scary, and challenging, and full of real or imagined risk.

All of which are necessary elements of a life lived in a fully inhabited, meaningful manner.

Life is like that. Even in the simple things. There are those who resent the need to go to a job every day, to have their time co-opted in a manner not exactly of their choosing (though I hope you are coming to realize that you can have choice in the matter). And there are those who even believe that the goal with a job is to work hard now so that they can eventually enjoy a relaxing retirement. Or win the lottery so they can lead a leisurely life.

But, as I pointed out earlier, too much leisure can lead just as inexorably into depression and discontentment as too much work, or work of the wrong kind.

Without challenges, we do not grow. Without growth, we atrophy. Going through the experience of being compelled to work, even in a job we don't love, can be valued in terms of the contrast it offers. For example, we know what we *don't* want. And we learn the difference between a day we've crafted for ourselves and a day we are obligated to. In this way, also, we love, and appreciate, and value those moments of joy that have an added depth because they have been constructed from all the effort it took to arrive there.

The greatest struggles, though, will not be the physical circumstances we find ourselves in. Whether they occur during our recreational times, or in our day-to-day lives. They will not be the cost of the plane ticket to Keflavik, Iceland. They will not be the miles of snow that must be crossed. They will not be hunger, or handicaps, or a dearth of opportunities, or poverty, or the schools we did or didn't go to, or where we live or work, or what job we have, or who our parents are. They will be the failure to believe in possibility, to imagine greater things, to think better thoughts, and to trust that those thoughts can steer one toward greater abundance and happiness.

This is a mental game. The greatest battles take place in our own minds.

CHAPTER TWELVE

GOING FOR
THE NEXT HANDHOLD

"Your pain is the breaking of the shell
that encloses your understanding.
Even as the stone of the fruit must break,
that its heart may stand in the sun,
so you must know pain.
And could you keep your heart in wonder
at the daily miracles of your life,
your pain would not seem less wondrous than your joy;
and you would accept the seasons of your heart,
even as you have always accepted
the seasons that pass over your fields."

-Kahlil Gibran

The above quote illustrates something profound: that the quality of your perspective can hold a major key to the quality of your life. Things, people, and circumstances are not just what they are; they are what we perceive them to be. What we see and how we see it is more about the person behind the eyes than about the images that are being taken in; not what is seen, but who is doing the seeing.

When we understand that our experiences are greatly influenced by our perspectives, it is easier to come to terms with the pain in our lives.

No life is free of pain. If we could have a God's eye view, we might even appreciate why that is. Pain and joy; life and death. Is it not the one that makes the other so precious? Is it not our experience of bitter winters that makes our hearts rejoice at the arrival of spring? Was it not the laborious trek through snow in Iceland that made the rest and respite afterward so comforting to me?

I believe strongly that it is important to feel all of our emotions, and not deny the validity or the reality of any of them. What I would suggest, though, is that we do have a choice about the perspective we want to take regarding the things that cause us discomfort or pain. Sometimes these choices can help us relax into a gentle and graceful acceptance of this "flip side of the coin" of life—in exactly the way illustrated by the Kahlil Gibran quote.

There are so many reasons why this is important. First, pain, and loss, and tragedy, and misfortune are inescapable in this world. But we need not let them *define* this world.

Likewise, when we are beset with these things, we need not let them define *us*.

The more we identify with the circumstances we believe have held us back or held us down in life, the less likely we are to rise above them, or succeed in spite of them. We allow ourselves to become victims of the past rather than architects of the future.

There is no life that is without some measure of sorrow, and the more we are able to view this aspect as having its place, as part of the richness of being alive, the more we are able to experience our joy fully and fearlessly.

Second, there can be a strange kind of beauty in death and loss. To have it teach us the depth of love; to help us reconcile our own mortality; to remind us of what is important, and to make a difference in this world, or in someone's life. To deepen our capacity to feel *everything*. Indeed, if we are to experience *life* holistically and richly, we cannot scrape away the undesirable bits, like peeling the edges of crust from a sandwich. There is an integrity and synthesis that must be preserved—and this requires everything that life delivers to us.

Third, there is probably not a one among us who hasn't witnessed the spectacle of a spoiled child: it is given everything it wants, and yet it cries out and flails about in the anguish of its seemingly unmet needs. An impertinent, demanding, irritating child. And, also, let me point out, a *miserable* child. No perspective. No understanding of how value is gained, or the benefits of self-control, or the pleasure of being occasionally distracted *away* from what one wants because one simply doesn't get it right away. Here is a child bereft of appreciation; in possession of no coping skills, and manifesting a general peevishness in all its interactions.

It is important and necessary to feel *want*, to experience *lack*, to know *disappointment*, because therein lies the impetus for us to struggle, and fight, and persevere, and learn, and grow, and get creative, and *evolve* as a human being. And, also, to become patient, and circumspect, and accepting. In these things we find satisfaction, confidence, meaning, and fulfillment. If we bypass them, we bypass our greatest potential.

So it is with pain and suffering.

When I had to have my old cat, Gigi, euthanized, I stayed with her while the needle was inserted, and she went into that eternal sleep. It was hard to do. There was riotous pain in my chest, but I was very certain that I wanted to stay with her.

I know a secret: it is an honor to be with something or someone when they pass. It can be a precious gift to be the final touch before they move on. So I let the pain pierce my heart, and I felt so blessed to feel that. So blessed to have loved her that much. To be someone that can love like that. What else can I do? Wish away that softness? Try not to be human? The best I can do—I know this, somehow, deep inside myself under the horror of it—is to cherish that feeling and that pain. And to know that it is valuable. That it is special, and priceless, and something to honor about myself—not something to wish away, or regret. This is something that has developed in me over time. Broadening, deepening. The things I know I am equal to now. I'm glad of that, and I wouldn't want to miss such things.

So many times, I have been struck by the poignancy of pain. I used to want to be tougher. It took a long time for me to see that sensitivity as a gift. When I was a child, I used to tell myself that when I got older, things wouldn't hurt so much—the loss of a friend, the death of a pet. Little did I know that when I got older the sensitivity would only sharpen, and the pain deepen.

Through a divorce and three miscarriages. Through the deaths of people I thought had yet many years to live. Through disappointment, and change, and regret, and just feeling like a rogue or misfit in a society with boundaries that did not fit my unconventional sensibilities, or the capacity and desires of my heart.

But this is who I am. How lucky for me! I am attuned to the heartbeat of life. I can feel it start, I can feel it race, I can feel it stop. Why would I suggest that I should not also feel it break?

When we come to a place where we can accept the pain, we no longer experience our joy with a sense of foreboding—always fearing the flip side of that joy. We can engage with it fully.

But as you are feeling that pain, be careful of your thoughts around it. Are you making the pain *mean* something? Something about you, or about your circumstances, or about your worth as a human being. A bit like my feeling like a wimp or a sissy because I felt so harmed by my sensitivity toward animals. It did *not* mean these things at all, but this was the meaning I had been attaching to it for many years.

As another example, think of someone discovering that their spouse is having an affair. Does the anguish they experience morph into self-doubt or self-loathing? Is the pain deeper because they begin to believe that these circumstances are suggesting something about *them?* About their ability to hold the interest of someone they love? Or, alternately (and, sometimes, simultaneously) does the pain now tell that person to deride, disrespect, and resent their spouse? Do they develop, out of this trauma, a belief that people are fundamentally dishonest, manipulative, or undeserving of trust?

It's interesting how this sort of thing can happen in a variety of ways, and we have to be careful about exaggerating or morphing the meaning of our experiences. If you are driving down the road and someone cuts you off, is your angry response a result *only* of what just happened? Or an accumulation of similar things happening to you? Suddenly, you are turning one person's bad behavior (or even a careless moment) into "Everyone is so rude!" and "Why is everything going wrong today?" And then we have relinquished our own agency in our lives to the demons of chance and circumstance.

Because, frankly, you cannot expect that nothing unexpected, or lousy, or unlucky will ever happen to you; so, understand that you're going to encounter pain. Let it happen. Feel it. Release it. Learn the lessons it has to teach.

This idea of embracing and feeling our pain would almost seem to go against everything I am teaching here, about rising up, and overcoming, and thinking higher thoughts. But, no. There is a refinement that must take place; a tempering of the steel, if you will. And the discomfort and lessons of pain are part of that tempering.

Consider any great figure in history: Winston Churchill, Mother Theresa, Nelson Mandela, Alexander the Great, Martin Luther King, Jr. It isn't just that they accomplished amazing feats; it's also what they had standing in their way. And it doesn't even have to be people so far removed, historically, from us. Think of some of those I mentioned earlier: Oprah Winfrey, J.K. Rowling, Michael Jordan, Tony Robbins—and a slew of others. This is part of the story. This is how we become our best selves and gain influence out in the world.

Maya Angelou said it beautifully: "You may encounter many defeats, but you must not be defeated. In fact, it may be necessary to encounter the defeats, so you can know who you are, what you can rise from, how you can still come out of it."

There will always be adversity. What will you do with that adversity? Who will you become as a result of it?

This is what stories are made of.

When you think of who you are and who you are becoming, you would do yourself a disservice to compare yourself to those who got where they are without the appearance of any adversity. What does it serve you to say, "I can't do what they did; I don't have the same advantages." Good! You have greater advantages—the chance to overcome obstacles and prove your mettle. Rumi says, "Where there is ruin, there is hope for a treasure."

If we take on the perspective that our difficulties are the reason we can't achieve the life we want, we miss out on the opportunity to view those same difficulties as the very things that allow us to grow stronger, and smarter, and tougher. Or to have an experience we wouldn't have otherwise had. They can become the reason we *succeed*; they don't have to be the reason we fail.

You can practice this in your everyday life. You don't have to wait for a crisis to come along to allow you to flex your perspective muscle. I'll let the following story serve as an example of how this works.

My job as a professor requires a rather long commute—not in miles, but in time because traffic in Southern California can be a real beast—and in the event of a wildfire (common at certain times of the year), a Santa Ana wind event (and heaven forbid these two things happen at the same time!), road construction/repair, or just a bad accident, that commute can morph from one hour into two or three.

Such times are terribly frustrating, but I also see them as opportunities to practice changing my perspective. So, on one particular day when a wildfire in the Cajon Pass threatened to turn my homeward commute into an exercise in impatience and anxiety, I decided to make some deliberate choices about how I was going to handle it.

After picking up my teenage son from school, we reluctantly hit the road for home. I was hopeful, at first, that the fire would turn out to be a minor one, and that traffic would unsnarl quickly.

While the first part of that hope was fulfilled, the second part was not.

One hour after leaving work, there was still no end in sight. Deciding to make an adventure of this misfortune, I hopped on a different freeway (it was a less-direct route home, but traffic flowed a little smoother) and found an In N Out restaurant. My son's mood brightened notably. Who cares about taking hours to get home when you can stop at In N Out on the way?

We ate cheeseburgers and fries in the car, listened to Imagine Dragons on the stereo, and I had my son use his traffic apps to find some updates. We talked, and joked, and laughed. Though we were on the road for more than another hour, it didn't seem like a burden at all. We were having fun and enjoying the change in our usual routine. But it only happened because I made a conscious choice to be aware of my perspective and to see what kind of difference it would make if I chose to see our situation as "an opportunity" or "an adventure" rather than an irritation.

Napoleon Hill, who wrote the legendary treatise *Think and Grow Rich*, said it this way, "Every negative event contains within it the seed of an equal or greater benefit." But you have to draw it out; you have to look for it and be open.

Having a multitude of experiences—joy, and pain, and struggle, and success—creates a life of rich detail and nuance. Again, think of yourself as the sculptor, as the creator of your own life. If you are the creator, what are the things that add color, and character, and depth to this life you are creating? I'm not suggesting you deliberately add in pain and suffering and irritations—what I'm suggesting is that you have an appreciation for what these can do for you.

If you are a parent, you may feel distressed when your child fails at something or is disappointed. But, at the same time, you know that they must have these experiences, or they will be handicapped by the lack of them.

How do we learn patience? Perseverance? Courage? We learn by trial. We learn through struggle. We learn when we meet with failure, and we try again. Setbacks are not bad, if you do not perceive them as such.

If you can take the long view, you might get a glimpse into why God or Universal intelligence designed life in the way it was designed. An elegant symmetry arises from what appears to be chaotic, in the convoluted and intricate connections of physical processes on Earth, and in the purposeful struggle of those who seek to survive and thrive. In the way that death is a natural part of a cycle that leads inevitably and inexorably into life again.

I recognize that in the daily moments of our lives, these "truths" do not sway us much. In part, I think, because we are always a little unsure of them. As I mentioned before, hindsight is 20/20, but we don't have the benefit of hindsight until the event is, well, behind us. And in the moment of struggle or disappointment, there is nothing but *that moment*—that way you feel as it all happens. And that way you feel projects itself into the future as far as you can see. As you lose out on the dream job you applied for; as you get broken up with for the umpteenth time; as you discover that you're not pregnant—or that you are. As you fail the bar exam, or get fired, or lose the championship, or get word that your father has cancer—or that you do, or your child does. Not only is the present moment a collection of seemingly unbearable circumstances, but we imagine these circumstances producing an equally unbearable future.

As far as your perception allows you to see, the only reality, and the only sure thing is whatever is in front of you now. And if that is something bad, or disappointing, or difficult, it may be hard to let your consciousness take in anything else. You develop a morbid fascination with destruction; your brain literally seems to dim the lights on the world around you. You feel yourself sinking. And since you cannot picture a future that is any different from your present, the tortured *now* takes on an omnipotent presence. And, therefore, you don't know how to change what you feel. You cannot draw from the future to ease your pain—you don't know the future. And your past may not have much to recommend it.

But what you are forgetting is that since you cannot know the future, you cannot know that it is bad. And you cannot say that you are being realistic by being pessimistic; by wallowing in your hurt and misfortune. What you probably can say (if you would let yourself contemplate this) is that if you do nothing to change your perception, and your character, and your potential, your future will probably look a lot like your past.

It doesn't have to, though. That's the beautiful thing. William Blake brilliantly wrote, "If the doors of perception were cleansed, everything would appear to man as it is—infinite." Meaning, infinite possibility. Infinite potential. What if you faced the future with that perspective? What if, when you sat down at the drawing board of your life, you understood that you could pretty much draw whatever you want?

And to take that a step further, if we understand Universal design, and that all things are connected—across space and time—then we can extrapolate that the changes we make today will affect our lives into the future and affect the lives of those we come in contact with. What kind of influence do you want to have? This is not a game of chance. The possibilities of the future are infinite, but your actions today are part of the selection process. So even in a crisis, bring your best to bear.

Remember what I said early on in this book about electromagnetic radiation? About how you are emitting it, and others are receiving it? Well, consider this: what if that energy you emit is based—at least in part—on your emotions? What if your emotions are influencing your thoughts (and vice versa)? There is research to support this. The Heartmath Institute specializes in this type of research, and in learning and sharing what can be done with it. Their studies have shown that your heart and brain are influencing each other, and these, in turn, are influencing the world around you.

As I mentioned before, we've all had that experience of being "tuned in" to someone. So, if you consider that the impact you are having, first, on yourself and, second, on everything else, will have implications for your future, (even beyond the obvious ones of "whatsoever a man soweth, that shall he also reap"—Galatians 6:7), then you might be inclined to monitor all of it a little more closely.

The future is not yet made, and you can influence the making of it. Further, the very things that would sometimes make us want to give up on life, are also the things that can make it more precious, or make your experience more valuable to others, or give you the tools by which you can fulfill your ultimate potential.

Don't you know it? Did you think you got to coast to your best self? If you did, it wouldn't be your best self. That's how it works.

This is not meant to discourage you, but to fortify you.

Always remember that the coin has two sides, and that the seasons change. That day gives way to night, and vice versa. If you are not manning the helm; if you are not choosing your perspective; if you are not consciously creating your existence, you will be tossed, and battered, and possibly broken.

The person who has saved up a stash of money does not worry when financial crisis occurs. They recognize this as the time when they get to invest at a low rate and get a high return later. When everyone else is just struggling to survive. This is what you can do for yourself. Store up equity; create a savings account of courage, and skills, and constructive habits. These things will springboard you when opportunity presents itself, and they will allow you to persevere in hope when times are tough.

I think sometimes we get the idea that life has somehow selected *us* to wreak its havoc upon. We look around and see everyone attaining that which we have struggled endlessly to have. But, again, this is a matter of perspective. We have only our own, and no one else's. What if Nelson Mandela believed that his life was over when he was thrown into prison? Isn't it interesting how we can look at him and almost take for granted that of course he had a huge influence? *Of course*, South Africa benefited from this man. But did *he* know that when he was sitting in prison? Certainly not. He could have died there. It was the most likely possibility. But he acted as if there was a chance he might live.

Think about that. What if you acted *as if there was a chance you might live?*

There is a popular idea that we should live each day as if it's our last—and I understand the concept behind that sentiment. It's a reminder that we never know how long we have on this earth, and we should spend that time on things that matter. Seeking out things we enjoy; spending time with loved ones. Accomplishing what we want to accomplish with a certain amount of urgency (which is very helpful, and I'll talk about this more in a little bit).

But the truth is, if I lived each day like it was my last, I wouldn't be sitting here writing right now. I would be sitting outside on the back porch in this beautiful evening with my friends and family and a glass of fine wine. And I think that's a wonderful way to spend time. But not all the time. And not every day. I don't want to live each day as if it's my last because there's a darn good chance that I'm going to live for another one. And another one. And another one. Yes, be present to what you have in *this* day and in *this* moment, because it is undeniably precious.

But we must also act as if there's a chance we might live.

I recently had the strange situation of forgetting my own age. It has happened rather frequently over the years, but in this particular year I had, for the entire year, considered myself to be a certain age. Toward the end of the year, I realized I was actually a year younger. Do you know what this did for me? *It made me feel as if I had regained a year of my life.* And I thought to myself, oh my goodness, what can I do with this whole, sacred year?

We should have this perspective about every year of our life.

What can I do with this whole, sacred year?

Because when you look at it like that, it appears as if it is finite; as if you've just got the *one*. And the funny thing about that is that it causes us to not squander it. Which I think is the whole point of the recommendation to live each day as if it's our last. In a way, you could wonder if this isn't exactly what God had in mind when He created death to coexist with life. The reality of death wakes us up to our living. Perhaps infinity is best served by dealing in the finite. You can imagine yourself with infinite potential, but you must start working toward it within finite chunks of time.

Do you see how this all adds up? Look at it again from these basics:

1. **You choose a vision for your life.**

2. **You implant the idea into your mind with repetitive thoughts and affirmations.**

3. **You focus on positive perspectives, seek out positive influences, and minimize negative thoughts and influences.**

4. **You choose characteristics you would like to instill or improve upon and you act in accordance with those (by setting your intention, training your thoughts, and rehearsing your actions).**

5. **You set goals that are in line with the vision of your life, and you take steps toward their fulfillment each day.**

6. **You discipline yourself to do the hard work in the direction of your dreams.**

7. **You choose a perspective that takes into consideration how the pain and struggle in your life can lead to your best self. ("Reject your sense of injury," says Marcus Aurelius, "and the injury itself disappears.")**

Take on this checklist as a challenge and watch how your life transforms. The biggest obstacle to your success is your failure to believe that it's possible. Move forward as if you have no doubt of the outcome— even if there are times when you *do* have doubt. And those times will arrive. Maybe sooner; maybe later. You are going to question if any of it is going to work. I know because I went through it, too. Starting a practice, creating a habit, dreaming big—and then telling myself, "Oh, who am I fooling? This isn't going to work."

There were times when I gave up, and then started again. But if I wasn't doing *this*—running this checklist—then what *was* I doing? Sitting around waiting for something to happen? Resigning myself to a life of less than what I had imagined? What did I have to lose, anyway? My sacrifice was the effort it took to dream, to plan, to set goals, and to be disciplined about working that plan and achieving those goals.

That word, "sacrifice," can have a heavy or negative connotation. But I love what my friend Matthew Winston says about it: "sacrifice and discipline is about becoming a *disciple* to your truer nature." Looking at it that way, it would be silly to *not* do it. To not make those sacrifices so that I could become who I wanted to be and do the thing that really mattered to me. To get to the end of my life, as I mentioned earlier, and say, "I didn't even go for it. I didn't even try that hard."

In life, we can sometimes feel like we're climbing a really steep cliff, and that just when we start to get pretty high, we tell ourselves that it's too dangerous and too uncertain to keep moving forward. So, we give up and slide back down.

Again and again, we do this.

One day we come to realize that sliding down is a choice, and that we could just keep going up. And one day, maybe we do keep going up. Past the point where we could safely let go and drop back down again. This is where it gets magical. When we stop thinking about what's beneath or behind us, and we start focusing on what's ahead of us: that glorious skyline; that lofty summit; that sweet air of freedom and accomplishment. When we commit to the process, and we understand that the only REAL choice left to us is to keep going for the next handhold…and the next… and the next….

CHAPTER THIRTEEN

THE METAMORPHOSIS

*"The cosmos is within us. We are made of star stuff.
We are a way for the universe to know itself."*

~Carl Sagan

A way for the universe to know itself. That's what you are. Why would you play small? Why would you think so little of yourself? You are the consciousness that gives validity to existence. You are the awareness without which anything that existed would not be known to exist. You are a life that has the ability to imagine, and with that ability the means to create the future.

What will the future look like?

You decide.

Because if you don't, someone else will. Armies and governments will. And you will resent the world they create, and you will lament that you have no power, and you will cry that the deck is always, *and has always been,* stacked against you. You fail to claim what power you do have because you are afraid it isn't enough, or that it doesn't matter. Or maybe you think you have no power. So the choice isn't made; the action isn't taken.

But how can you know? How can you know that the moves you make, and that the person you become as a result of those moves will not lead to a perfect positioning of the stepping-stones on your path?

The truth is, you don't know. But which future would you rather shoot for? The one you had a hand in, or the one that gets handed to you?

There will come a time in your journey when the doubts will assail you far less frequently, you will have successes to show for your work and your perseverance, your feeling of momentum will be greater than your feeling of inertia, and your confidence will soar.

This could happen in one area that you're working on, or it could happen in your life, at large. Ultimately, you want all these gears to work together.

It's a bit like driving a car with a manual transmission. When you are first learning, each of the separate functions and actions that must take place seem awkward or even downright difficult. The level of concentration needed just to get the car to move forward without stalling seems ridiculous. Then, add in the brake, the gearshift, and all the distractions and hazards of the road itself, and the task can seem daunting, to say the least!

Once the basic task of using the clutch, brake pedal, gas pedal, and gear box in the right order and with the right timing is accomplished, it is handily given over to long-term memory and these moves becomes automatic. You can focus on the changing conditions of the road, and completely de-focus on how to manipulate the gears. It's quite astonishing, really, how the actions that needed your *complete* focus when you were first learning them, end up needing the *least* amount of your focus once they are learned. They become habitual and, therefore, easy.

This is very similar to what happens in our brains once we have mastered the "training" of how we want them to work. At first, it seems overwhelming. Changing the old pathways inside our minds that have always guided our thoughts, actions, and belief systems. We must be conscious of our thoughts *a lot* at first.

This can be quite difficult because you are going against years and years of engrained thinking and acting. All the things you have told yourself that are not so good have to be changed. And you have to *remember* to notice them, and to change them.

Additionally, you are trying to teach yourself a new and different way of being. More courageous, perhaps. More disciplined. Whatever those characteristics are that you would like to become a part of your identity. These goals require, then, an additional level of reminders, attention, and awareness. You are writing in your journal, thinking about your authentic self and your authentic talents and desires; you are making plans—writing, re-writing, revising—and then creating goals around those plans. And, in the meantime, you want to remember to choose your perspective, and not let the dips and turns of life shake your resolve or encourage you to focus on your circumstances over your personal wherewithal.

You want to constantly bring into your mind the image of who you want to *be*. Can you feel yourself responding as this other being? The *you* who makes people feel relaxed. The *you* who listens attentively and responds with thoughtful care. The *you* who knows how to call up your courage when fear leaps into your path.

Do you walk away from your various interactions with the sense that you were kind, honest, and engaged? What is the vibe you want to leave in the air when you walk out of a room? How do you want to challenge others to be *their* best selves, as well, and to inhabit each scenario as their own, authentic being? Think about this. Who you want to be. Where you want to go. Over and over. You want to see it, feel it, become it.

All of this can seem like too much is being asked of you but, really, it's just a lack of rehearsal. It just hasn't been fleshed-out yet. Like showing up for a speech without getting enough practice in. I want you to realize that it's normal, and it's ok. When you deep-clean a house, for example, it looks worse before it looks better. These things that start out so messy and difficult will begin to take shape. Again, let me remind you—you are sculpting your own self, and your own life. If you start off with an unformed lump of clay, it's not going to look like much. You're going to start uncovering the beauty hidden in that lump of clay, but it's not going to appear immediately. It takes time. It takes effort. It takes not giving up.

One day you will realize that you are irrevocably on the path to success, or your best life, or your authentic self, when you become tenaciously focused on your vision, and your sense and awareness of your true self, and when you refuse to let anything derail you. When your faith can hold up under your fear, and you have the sense that the future is malleable, and that *you* are shaping it.

What does this look like?

You will have a very clear and detailed idea in your mind about what you want your life to look like. The work that is important to you, the pleasures that are meaningful, the personal traits you can be proud of.

You will value the pieces of yourself that are uniquely *you*. This may be quite different from a time when, perhaps, you wanted to disown those parts. Or when you thought they weren't special or important.

You will have established habits that ensure you have the right mindset, and that you are making progress toward your goals.

You will no longer entertain thoughts like, "What if I can't do this?" Or, "What if this doesn't work?" Not that you will never be *inclined* to have those thoughts, but you will push them aside and go for the next handhold. Onward and upward. Your thoughts will be more on what you *can* do than on what you *can't* do. You will know how to exchange one for the other.

In your mind, you will only and always see success. You will *purge* your mind of any thoughts that try to derail you. You will have learned how to do this. You will become highly focused. Your faith will be strong because you have tools, and experience, and the ability to manage your thoughts and focus. You will become resolute about your vision and your path. You will set clear boundaries all around you, protecting your time, your inner knowledge, your peace of mind, and your trust in your self-awareness.

You will take the actions that move you toward the goal, and when an obstacle comes, you will search for ways around it until you find one.

You will do this over and over. Indefatigably. Always holding the vision in front of you, and your internal compass at the ready.

Once you reach this point, success is assured. You will not fail.

What's quite interesting and exciting is that, even before you reach this point when all the gears are working together and driving you toward the big dream, you can feel this same sense of inevitable success in some of the smaller areas. It's amazing because you learn to recognize what it feels like, and you can duplicate the actions that got you there. This is why one often hears stories of self-made millionaires who lost their fortunes and were able to start over again from scratch and regain their millions in just a few years.

Once you know how to do it, you know how to do it.

So, understand, all the struggle and effort is leading to something. And on the way, there is a learning process taking place that will serve you massively for the rest of your life.

Undertake this challenge I have set out for you and you will not be the same person in the end. You will be like a caterpillar metamorphosizing. The butterfly that emerges will still be *you*—but it will be the best, most beautiful version of *you* that you could imagine.

And you will imagine it. That's what you start off with—imagining. And one day, you will have chipped away at and carved through all the extraneous stuff that hides your authenticity. All the ill-gotten beliefs that rob you of your confidence and your purpose. You will have deliberately put aside the thoughts that do not serve you and you will have replaced them with a blueprint of brilliance. You will come to realize that you are truly living into your infinite potential.

You will have excavated, brushed off, and polished the astonishing light of your own being. It has always been there. A diamond doesn't become a diamond only when it is cut and polished—that is simply when it shines the brightest. It has always been a diamond.

And so it is with each and every one of us.

You can be proof-positive that we all have the ability to transform our lives, to create reality out of something seemingly impossible, to define and reach our highest potential, and to create a future that we imagined into existence. It's all there for you. You have the capacity.

Believe in your brilliance and go share it with the world. Be the one who shows others what can happen when you believe you are the architect of your own future, and when you have the courage to model and build the life of your dreams.

It is your birthright. It is a part of being conscious and being human.

*"And above all, watch with glittering eyes
the whole world around you because the greatest secrets
are always hidden in the most unlikely places.
Those who don't believe in magic will never find it."*

-Roald Dahl

www.ingramcontent.com/pod-product-compliance
Lightning Source LLC
Chambersburg PA
CBHW061732050726
47598CB00002B/455